I0805332

# ESSENTIAL ELEMENTS for Band

## COMPREHENSIVE BAND METHOD

TIM LAUTZENHEISER • JOHN HIGGINS • CHARLES MENGHINI
PAUL LAVENDER • TOM C. RHODES • DON BIERSCHENK

Band is...

**M** aking music with a family of lifelong friends.

**U** nderstanding how commitment and dedication lead to success.

**S** haring the joy and rewards of working together.

**I** ndividuals who develop self-confidence.

**C** reativity—expressing yourself in a universal language.

Band is...**MUSIC!**

*Strike up the band,*
Tim Lautzenheiser

### HISTORY OF THE CLARINET

In 1690, the German instrument maker Johann Denner invented the clarinet by transforming the double reed "chalumeau" (shall-you-mo) into a single reed instrument. Since the chalumeau could only play notes in a low range, he added a "register key" to allow his new instrument to play higher notes. The word clarinet comes from the Italian word *clarino*, used for an older type of high-pitched trumpet. Today the low range of the clarinet is still called the "chalumeau register," because of the low notes of the original chalumeau.

By the 1840's, two French instrument makers named Klosé and Buffet had created a clarinet fingering system modeled after the flute key system designed by Boehm. Nearly all clarinets today are made with the Boehm system.

The clarinet family includes the B♭ Clarinet, the A Clarinet (used in some orchestra music), the B♭ Bass Clarinet, the E♭ Soprano and Alto Clarinets, the E♭ Contrabass Clarinet and B♭ Contrabass Clarinet. Fingerings are virtually the same for all clarinets, making it possible for a clarinetist to play any of the instruments. As one of the primary instruments in the sound of a concert band, clarinets play melodies, harmonies and solos.

Mozart, Brahms, Weber, Bartok and Hindemith are among the important composers who have featured clarinets in their writing. Some famous clarinetists include Richard Stoltzman, Benny Goodman, Eddie Daniels, Stanley Drucker, John Bruce Yeh, Sabine Meyer, Anthony McGill and Doreen Ketchens.

To create an account, visit:
**www.essentialelementsinteractive.com**

Student Activation Code
E1CL-4886-8799-2534

ISBN 979-835012059-2
Copyright © 1999, 2004, 2025 by HAL LEONARD LLC
International Copyright Secured All Rights Reserved

HAL•LEONARD®
A Muse Group Company

# THE BASICS

## Posture

Sit on the edge of your chair, and always keep your:

- Spine straight and tall
- Shoulders back and relaxed
- Feet flat on the floor

## Breathing & Airstream

Breathing is a natural thing we all do constantly. To discover the correct airstream to play your instrument:

- Place the palm of your hand near your mouth.
- Inhale deeply through the corners of your mouth, keeping your shoulders steady. Your waist should expand like a balloon.
- Slowly whisper "too" as you gradually exhale air into your palm.

The air you feel is the airstream. It produces sound through the instrument. Your tongue is like a faucet or valve that releases the airstream.

## Producing The Essential Tone

Your embouchure *(ahm´-bah-shure)* is your mouth's position on the mouthpiece of the instrument. A good embouchure takes time and effort, so carefully follow these steps for success:

### REED PLACEMENT

- Put the thin end of the reed in your mouth to moisten it thoroughly.
- Looking at the flat side of the mouthpiece, the ligature screws extend to your right. Slide the ligature up with your thumb.
- Place the flat side of the reed against the mouthpiece under the ligature.
- Lower the ligature and position the reed so that only a hairline of the mouthpiece can be seen above the reed.
- Gently tighten the ligature screws.

### EMBOUCHURE

- Moisten your lips and roll the lower lip over your bottom teeth.
- Firm the corners of your mouth like a slightly puckered smile.
- Stretch your chin downward.
- Place the mouthpiece on your lower lip so that the reed extends about 1/2 inch into your mouth. Place upper teeth on top of the mouthpiece.
- Close your mouth around the mouthpiece. Keep the corners of the mouth firm and the chin pointing downward.

## Taking Care Of Your Instrument

Before putting your instrument back in its case after playing, do the following:

- Remove the reed, wipe off excess moisture and return it to the reed case.
- Remove the mouthpiece and wipe the inside with a clean cloth. Once a week, wash the mouthpiece with warm tap water. Dry thoroughly.
- Drop a weighted chamois or cotton swab into the bell and pull it out through the barrel.
- Carefully twist off the barrel and dry off any additional moisture. Place it in the case.
- Gently twist the upper and lower sections apart, with the bell still attached. Place the upper section in the case.
- Remove the bell and place the bell and lower section back into the case.
- As you put each piece back in the case, check to be sure they are dry.
- Your case is designed to hold only specific objects. If you try to force anything else into the case, it may damage your instrument.

## MOUTHPIECE WORKOUT

Form your embouchure around the mouthpiece, and take a deep breath without raising your shoulders. Whisper "too" and gradually exhale your full airstream. Strive for an even tone.

## Getting It Together

*If you just played the MOUTHPIECE WORKOUT, begin by carefully removing the reed. Otherwise, take the reed from its case.*

**Step 1** Put the thin end of the reed into your mouth to moisten it thoroughly while assembling your instrument. If needed, rub a small amount of cork grease on all corks. Clean hands.

**Step 2** Hold the lower section in the palm of your left hand, with the key work facing up. Do not put any pressure on the long rod. Pick up the bell with your right hand and gently twist it onto the cork of the lower section.

**Step 3** Hold the upper section in your right hand so you can depress the lower of the two open rings with your second finger. Gently twist the upper section into the lower section. Check that the bridge key on the upper section crosses directly over its connector on the lower section. The tone holes of the two sections should be aligned.

**Step 4** Hold your instrument in your left hand, near the top of the upper section. Pick up the barrel in your right hand and gently twist its larger end onto the top of the upper section.

**Step 5**
Twist the mouthpiece into the barrel. The flat side of the mouthpiece should form a straight line with the register key and thumb rest. Place the reed on the mouthpiece (see page 2).

**Step 6**
With your right thumb under the thumb rest and left thumb on the thumb key, use the pads of your fingers to cover the tone holes. Your fingers should curve naturally. Bring the clarinet up as shown on the left:

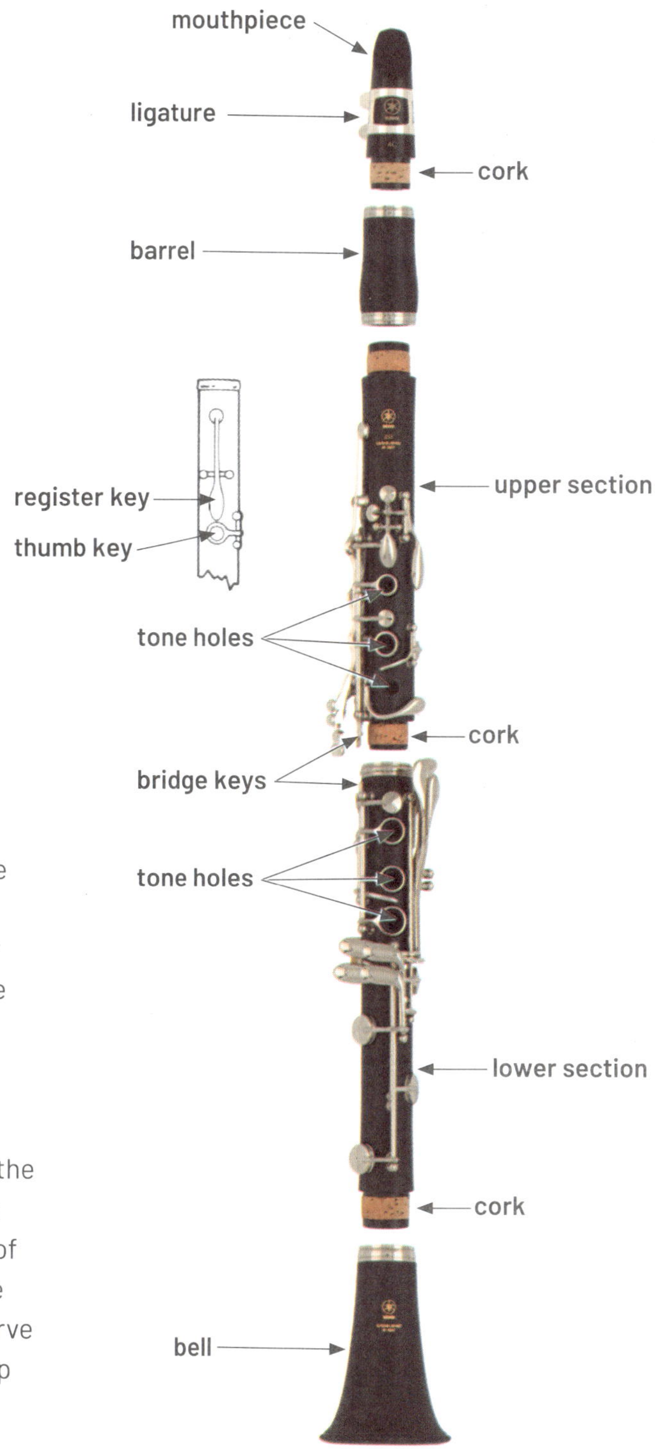


*The student shown is a member of the Milwaukee Youth Symphony Orchestra.*

## READING MUSIC

Identify and draw each of these symbols:

### Music Staff

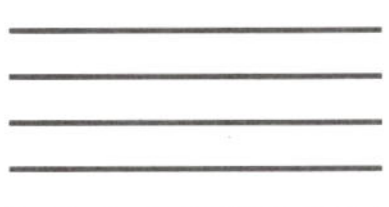

The **music staff** has 5 lines and 4 spaces where notes and rests are written.

### Ledger Lines

**Ledger lines** extend the music staff. Notes on ledger lines can be above or below the staff.

### Measures & Bar Lines

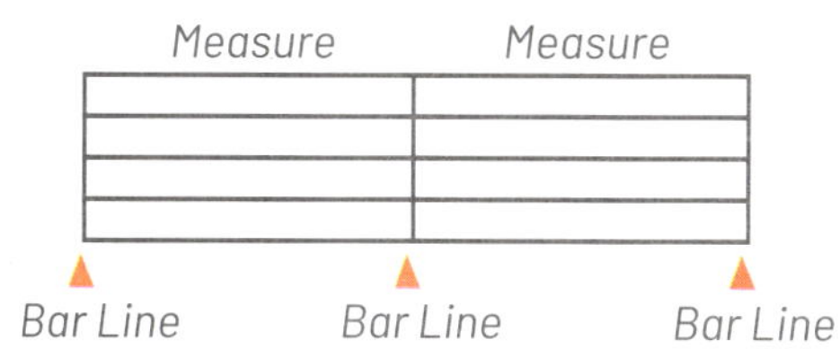


**Bar lines** divide the music staff into **measures**.

## Long Tone

To begin, we'll use a special "Long Tone" note. Hold the tone until your teacher tells you to rest. Practice long tones each day to develop your sound.

## 1. THE FIRST NOTE

Hold each long tone until your teacher tells you to rest.

**G**

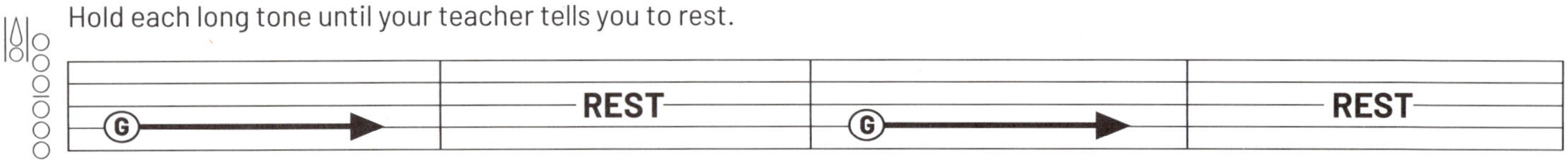


*"G" is played **open**. Keep your fingers relaxed and curved above the tone holes.*

### The Beat

The **beat** is the pulse of music, and like your heartbeat it should remain very steady. Counting aloud and foot-tapping help us maintain a steady beat. Tap your foot **down** on each number and **up** on each "&."

**One beat = 1 &**

↓ ↑

### Notes & Rests

**Notes** tell us how high or low to play by their placement on a line or space of the music staff, and how long to play by their shape. **Rests** tell us to count silent beats.

**Quarter Note = 1 beat**

**Quarter Rest = 1 silent beat**

## 2. COUNT AND PLAY

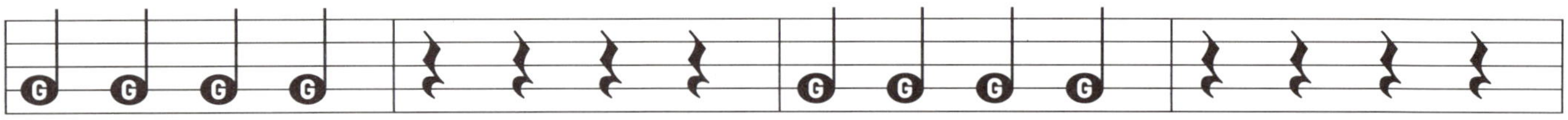


*Count:* 1 & 2 & 3 & 4 & 1 & 2 & 3 & 4 & 1 & 2 & 3 & 4 & 1 & 2 & 3 & 4 &

*Tap:* ↓ ↑ ↓ ↑ ↓ ↑ ↓ ↑ ↓ ↑ ↓ ↑ ↓ ↑ ↓ ↑ ↓ ↑ ↓ ↑ ↓ ↑ ↓ ↑ ↓ ↑ ↓ ↑ ↓ ↑ ↓ ↑

## 3. A NEW NOTE

Look for the fingering diagram with each new note.

**F**

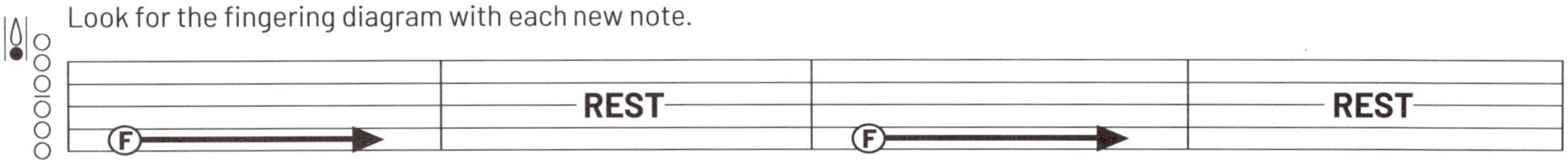


▲ *The black circles tell you which tone holes to cover or keys to press. "F" is played with the **left thumb**.*

## 4. TWO'S A TEAM

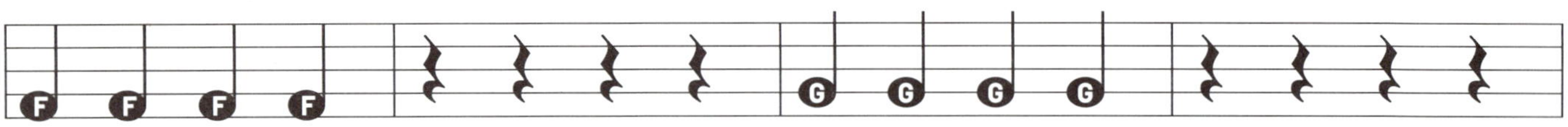


*Count & Tap:* 1 & 2 & 3 & 4 & 1 & 2 & 3 & 4 & 1 & 2 & 3 & 4 & 1 & 2 & 3 & 4 &

## 5. HEADING DOWN

Practice long tones on each new note.

**E**

## 6. MOVING ON UP

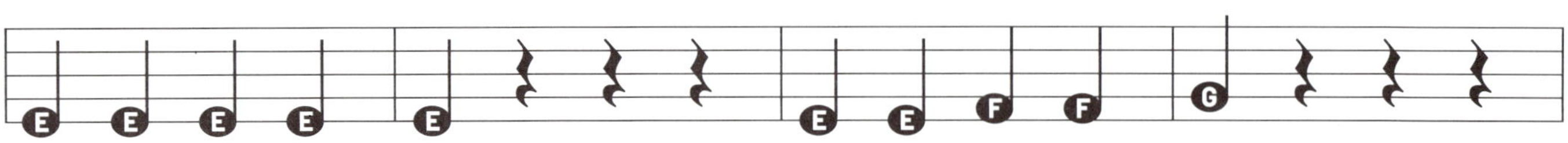


*Count & Tap:* 1 & 2 & 3 & 4 & 1 & 2 & 3 & 4 & 1 & 2 & 3 & 4 & 1 & 2 & 3 & 4 &

*See inside front cover for information on accessing instructional videos.*

**Double Bar**  indicates the end of a piece of music.

**Repeat Sign** 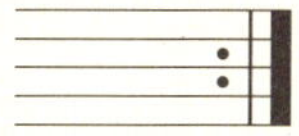 Without stopping, play once again from the beginning.

## 7. THE LONG HAUL

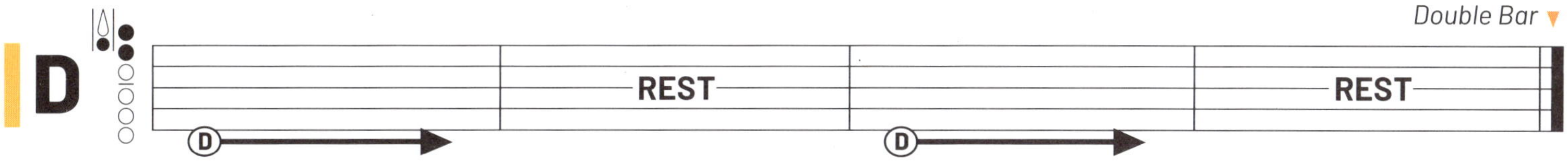


## 8. FOUR BY FOUR

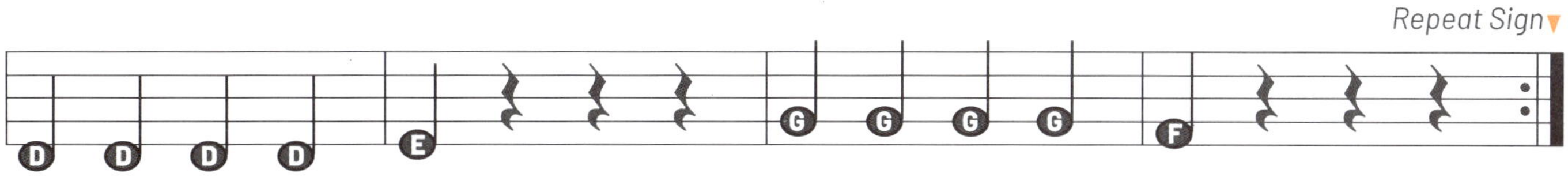


*Count & Tap:* 1 & 2 & 3 & 4 & 1 & 2 & 3 & 4 & 1 & 2 & 3 & 4 & 1 & 2 & 3 & 4 &

## 9. TOUCHDOWN

## 10. THE FAB FIVE

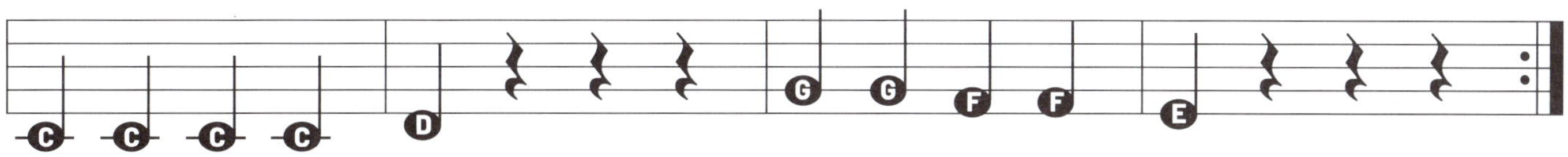


1 & 2 & 3 & 4 & 1 & 2 & 3 & 4 & 1 & 2 & 3 & 4 & 1 & 2 & 3 & 4 &

### Treble Clef

(G Clef) indicates the position of note names on a music staff: Second line is G.

### Time Signature

indicates how many beats per measure and what kind of note gets one beat.

= **4 beats** per measure
= **Quarter** note gets one beat

### Note Names

Each note is on a line or a space of the staff. These note names are indicated by the Treble Clef.

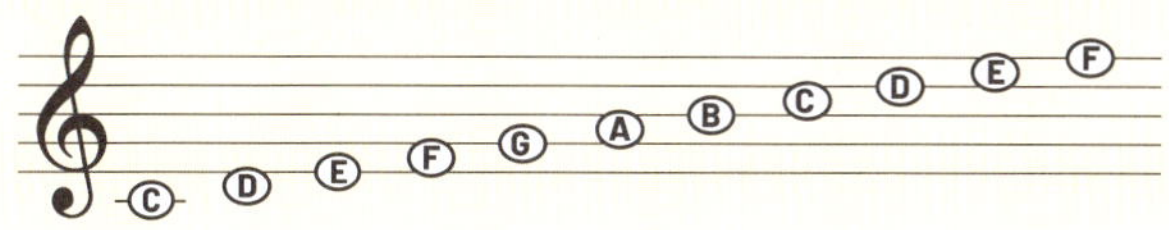


**Sharp** ♯ raises the note and remains in effect for the entire measure.
**Flat** ♭ lowers the note and remains in effect for the entire measure.
**Natural** ♮ cancels a flat (♭) or sharp (♯) and remains in effect for the entire measure.

THEORY

## 11. READING THE NOTES *Compare this to exercise 10, THE FAB FIVE.*

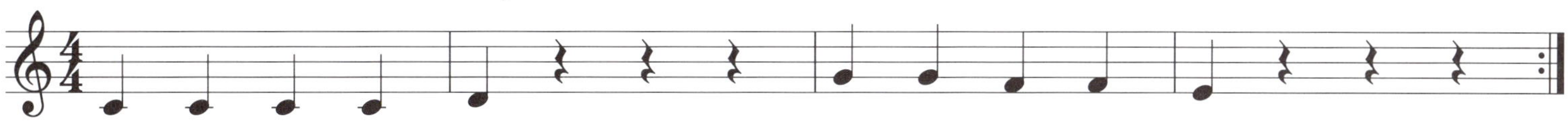

1 & 2 & 3 & 4 & 1 & 2 & 3 & 4 & 1 & 2 & 3 & 4 & 1 & 2 & 3 & 4 &

## 12. FIRST FLIGHT

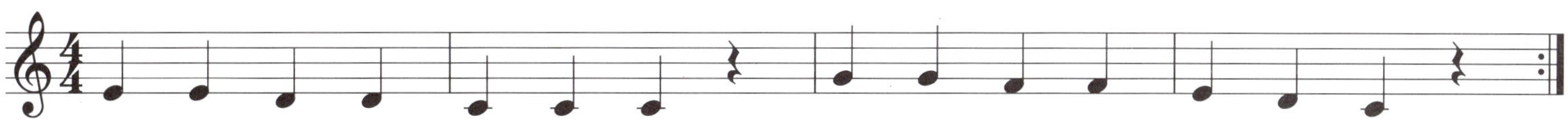

## 13. ESSENTIAL ELEMENTS QUIZ *Fill in the remaining note names before playing.*

C D E ___ ___ ___ ___ ___ ___ ___ ___ ___ ___ ___ ___ ___

## Notes In Review

Memorize the fingerings for the notes you've learned:

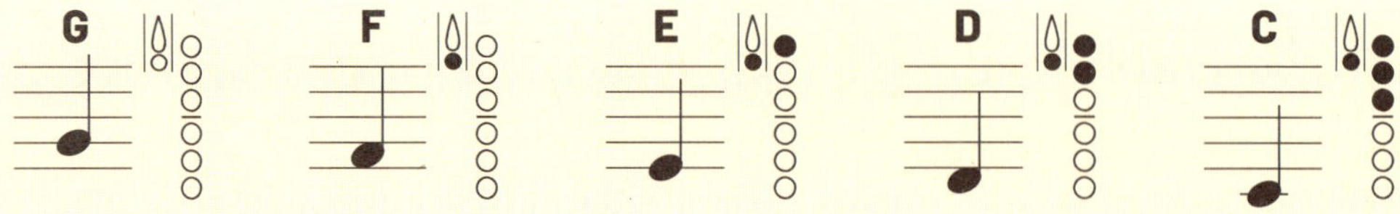


### 14. ROLLING ALONG

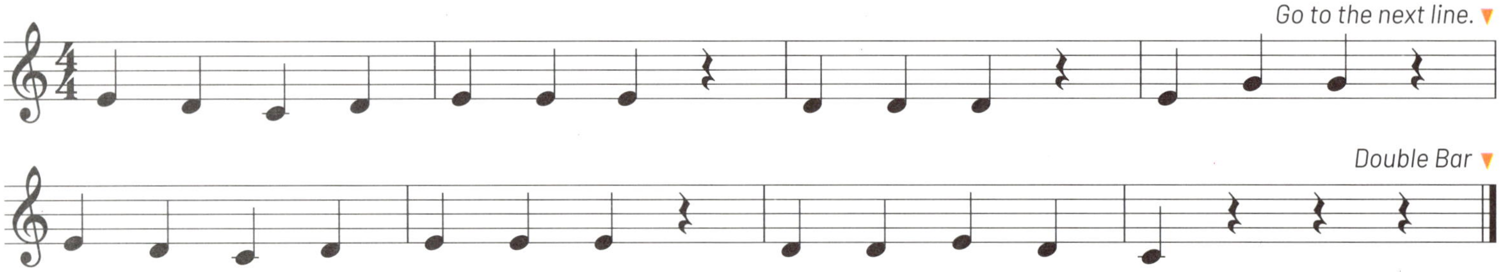


## Half Note

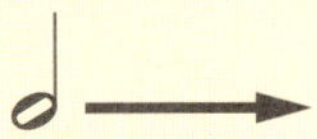

= 2 Beats

1 & 2 &

## Half Rest

= 2 Silent Beats

1 & 2 &

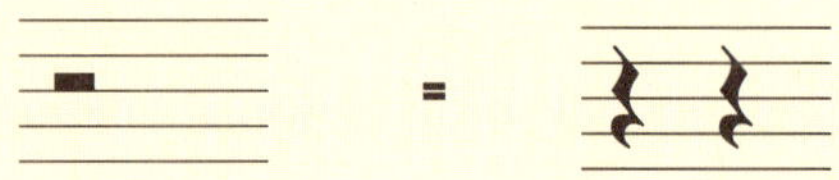

### 15. RHYTHM RAP *Clap the rhythm while counting and tapping.*

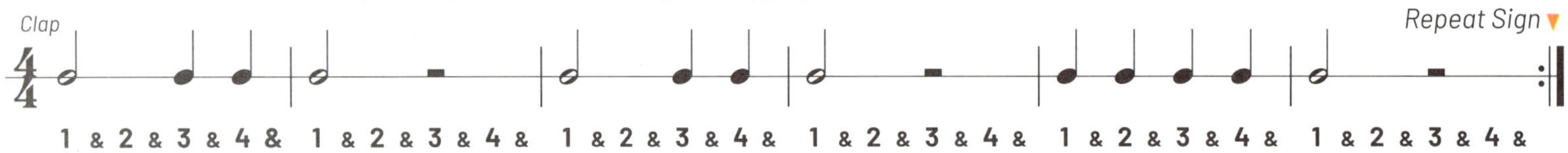


### 16. THE HALF COUNTS

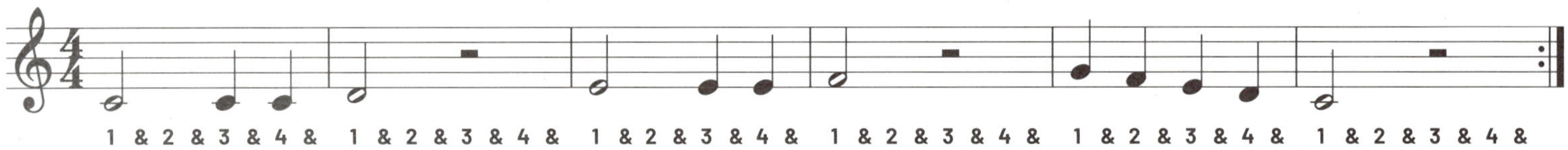


### 17. HOT CROSS BUNS *Check your embouchure and hand position.*

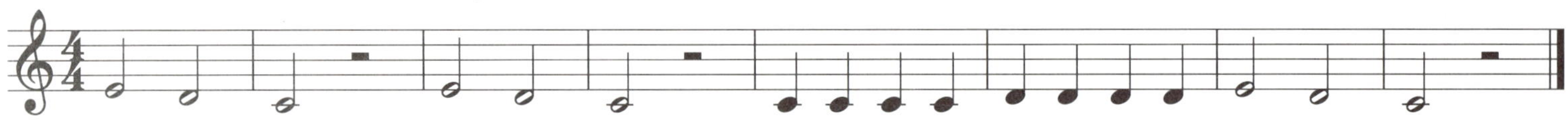

## Breath Mark ’

Take a deep breath through your mouth after you play a full-length note.

### 18. GO TELL AUNT RHODIE

American Folk Song

### 19. ESSENTIAL ELEMENTS QUIZ *Using the note names and rhythms below, draw your notes on the staff before playing.*

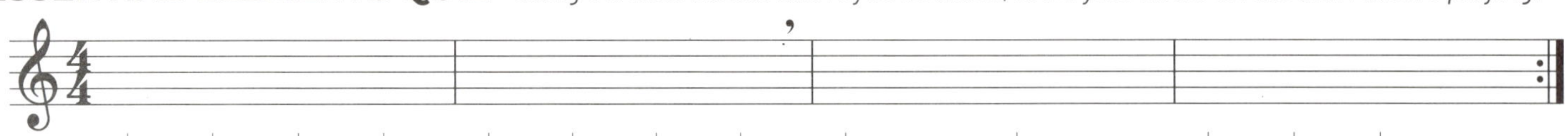

F G F E F E D C D E F E F

## Whole Note

o ——→ = 4 Beats

1 & 2 & 3 & 4 &

## Whole Rest

= A Whole Measure of Silent Beats

1 & 2 & 3 & 4 &

**Whole Rest**

hangs from a staff line.

**Half Rest**

sits on a staff line.

### 20. RHYTHM RAP *Clap the rhythm while counting and tapping.*

1 & 2 & 3 & 4 & 1 & 2 & 3 & 4 & 1 & 2 & 3 & 4 & 1 & 2 & 3 & 4 & 1 & 2 & 3 & 4 & 1 & 2 & 3 & 4 &

### 21. THE WHOLE THING

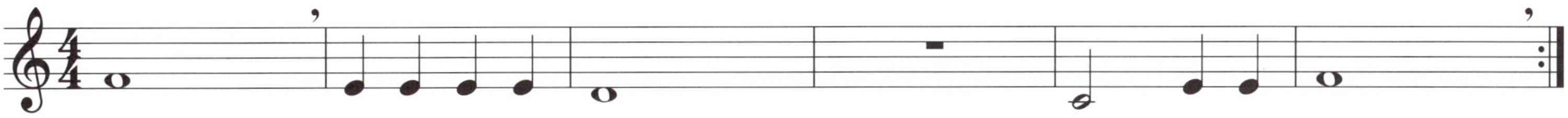

1 & 2 & 3 & 4 & 1 & 2 & 3 & 4 & 1 & 2 & 3 & 4 & 1 & 2 & 3 & 4 & 1 & 2 & 3 & 4 & 1 & 2 & 3 & 4 &

## Duet

A composition with two different parts, played together.

### 22. SPLIT DECISION – Duet

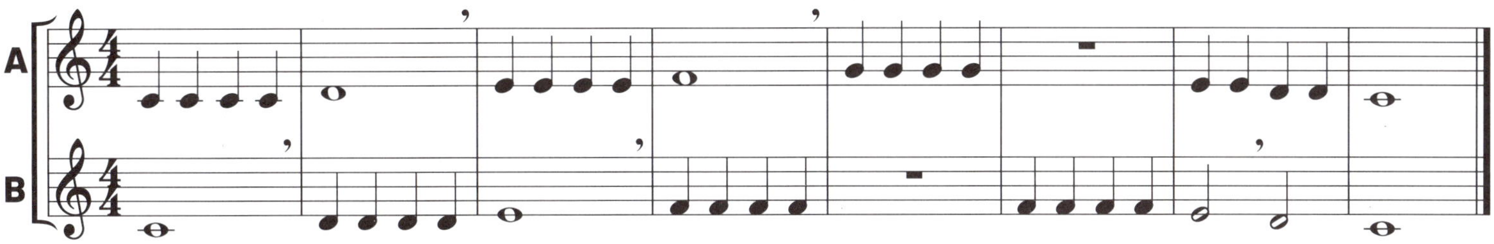


## Key Signature

The **Key Signature** tells us which notes to play with sharps (♯) or flats (♭) throughout the music. Your Key Signature indicates the *Key of C* (no sharps or flats).

THEORY

### 23. MARCH STEPS

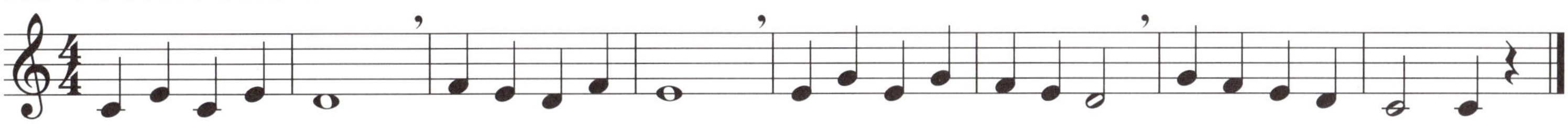

### 24. LISTEN TO OUR SECTIONS

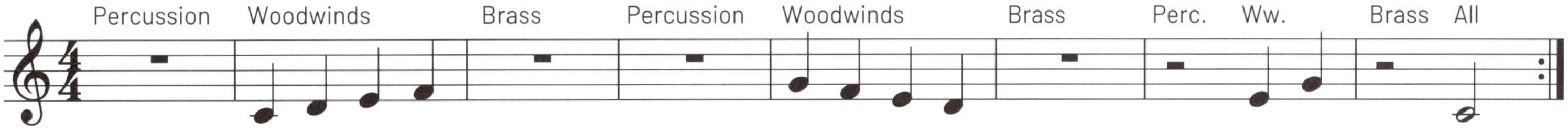


### 25. LIGHTLY ROW

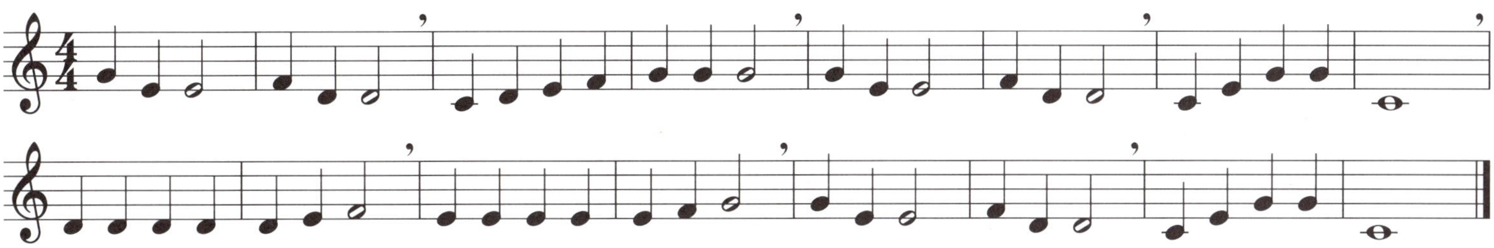

### 26. ESSENTIAL ELEMENTS QUIZ *Draw in the bar lines before you play.*

**Fermata** 𝄐 Hold the note (or rest) longer than normal.

## 27. REACHING HIGHER – New Note

*Practice long tones on each new note.*

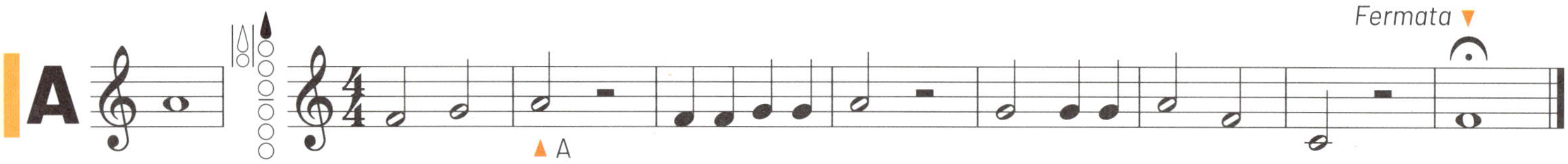


## 28. AU CLAIRE DE LA LUNE

French Folk Song

## 29. REMIX

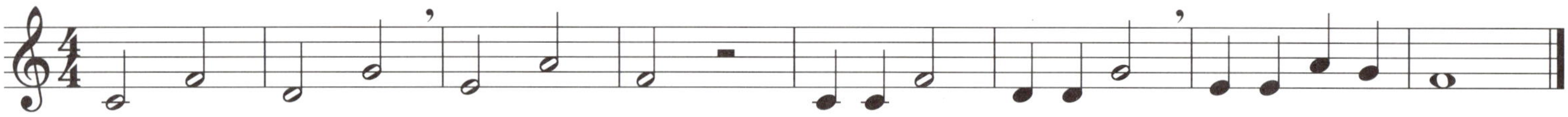

THEORY

**Harmony** Two or more notes played together. Each combination forms a *chord.*

## 30. LONDON BRIDGE – Duet

English Folk Song

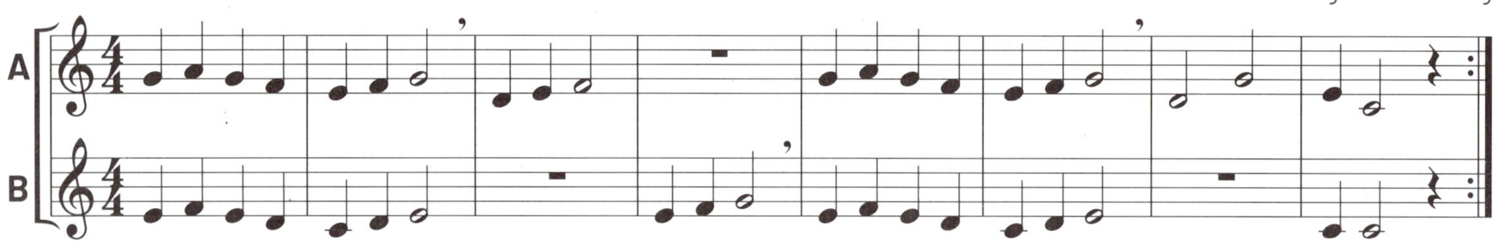


HISTORY

Austrian composer **Wolfgang Amadeus Mozart** (1756–1791) was a child prodigy who started playing professionally at age six, and lived during the time of the American Revolution. Mozart's music is melodic and imaginative. He wrote more than 600 compositions during his short life, including a piano piece based on the famous song, "Twinkle, Twinkle, Little Star."

## 31. A MOZART MELODY

Adaptation

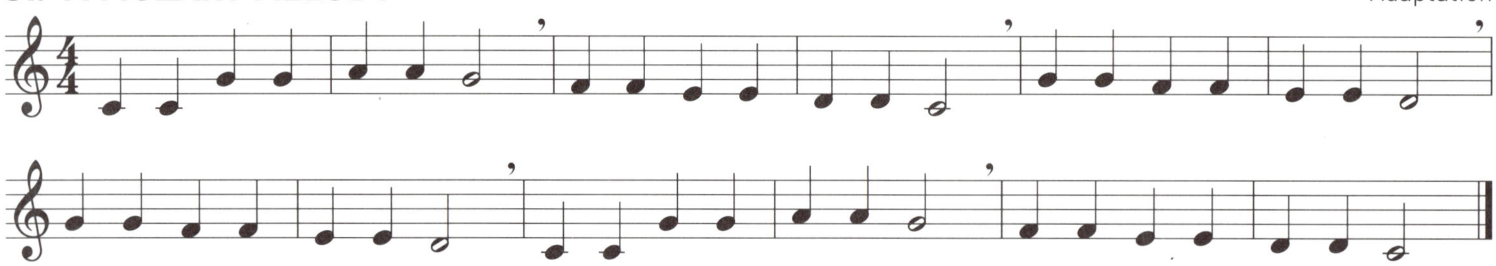

## 32. ESSENTIAL ELEMENTS QUIZ

*Draw these symbols where they belong and write in the note names before you play:*

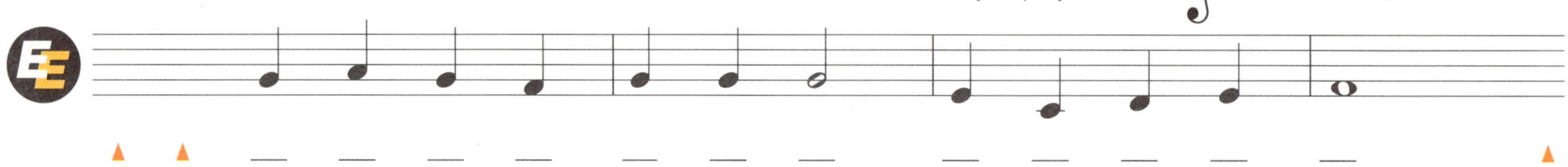

## 33. DEEP POCKETS – New Note

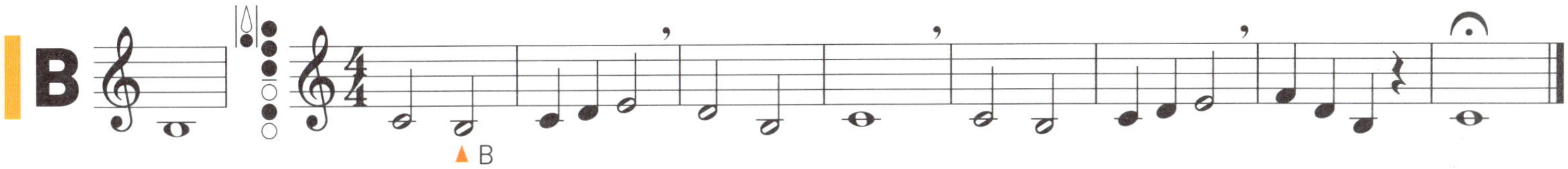


## 34. DOODLE ALL DAY

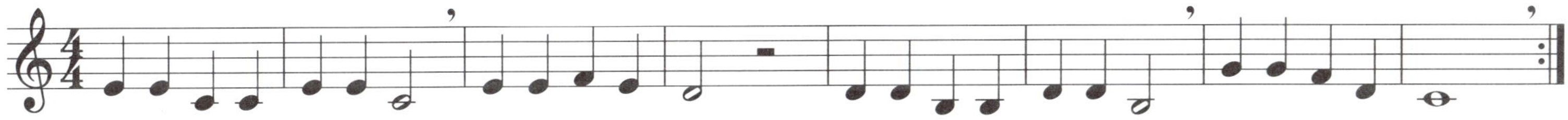

## 35. JUMP ROPE

**Pick-Up Notes** One or more notes that come before the first *full* measure.
The beats of Pick-Up Notes are subtracted from the last measure.

## 36. A-TISKET, A-TASKET

**Dynamics** ***f*** - *forte* (play loudly) ***mf*** - *mezzo forte* (play moderately loud) ***p*** - *piano* (play softly)
Remember to use full breath support to control your tone at all dynamic levels.

## 37. LOUD AND SOFT

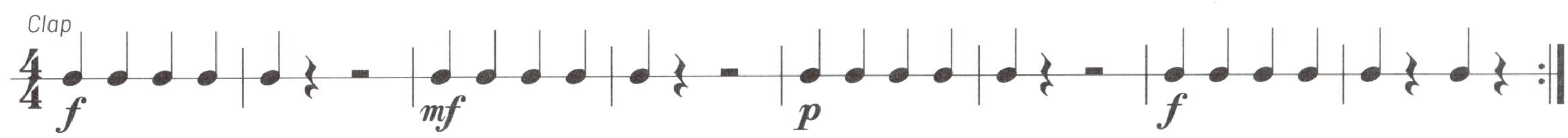


## 38. JINGLE BELLS *Keep your fingers close to the keys, curved naturally.*

J. S. Pierpont

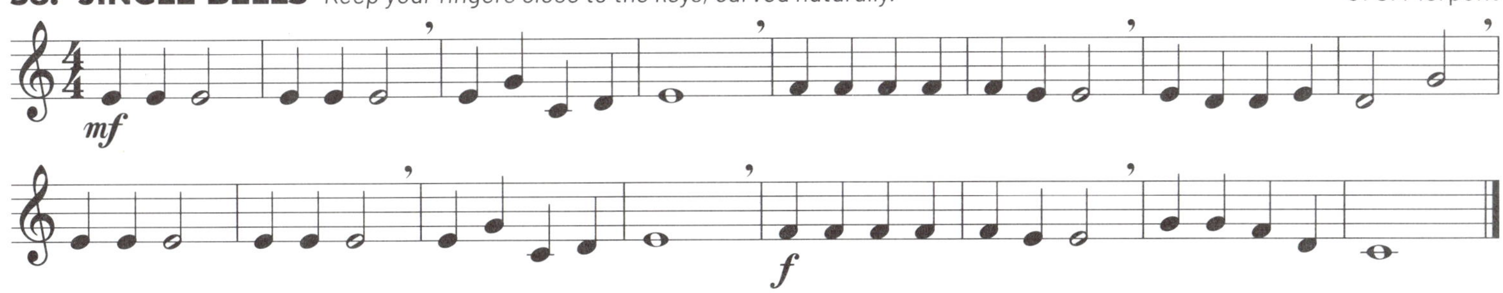


## 39. MY DREYDL *Use full breath support at all dynamic levels.*

Traditional Hanukkah Song

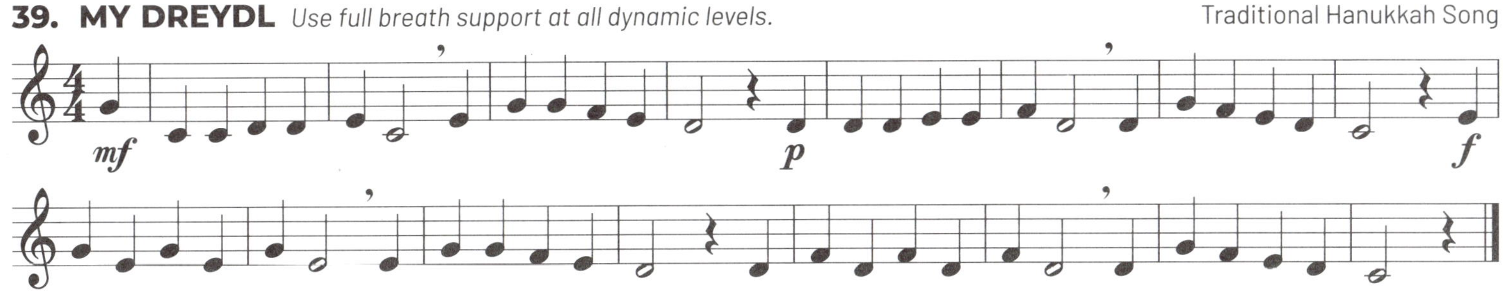

## Eighth Notes

Each Eighth Note = ½ Beat
2 Eighth Notes = 1 Beat
*Play on down and up taps.*

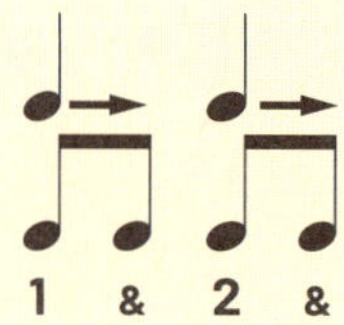


Two or more Eighth Notes have a *beam* across the stems.

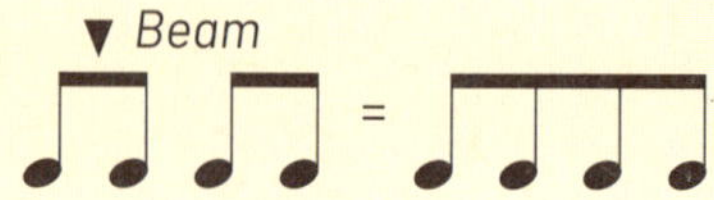


### 40. RHYTHM RAP *Clap the rhythm while counting and tapping.*

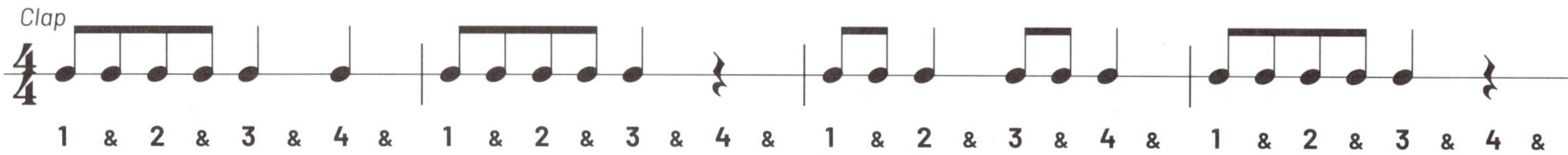


### 41. EIGHTH NOTE JAM

### 42. SKIP TO MY LOU

American Folk Song

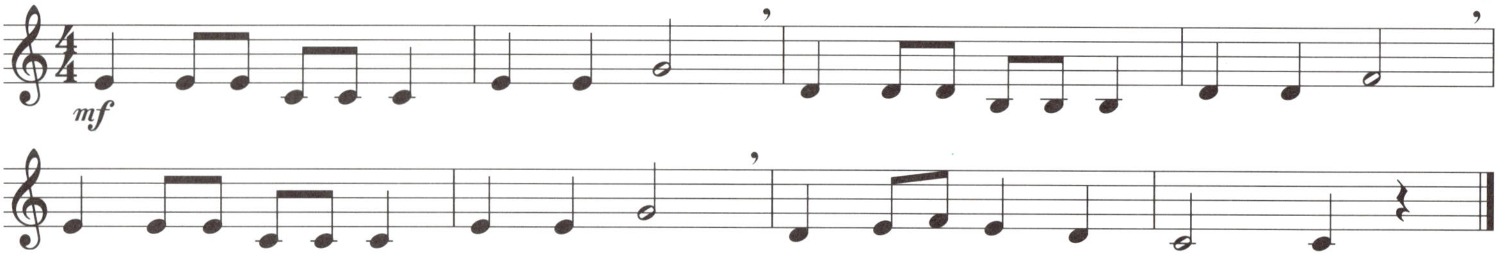


### 43. LONG, LONG AGO *Good posture improves your sound. Always sit straight and tall.*

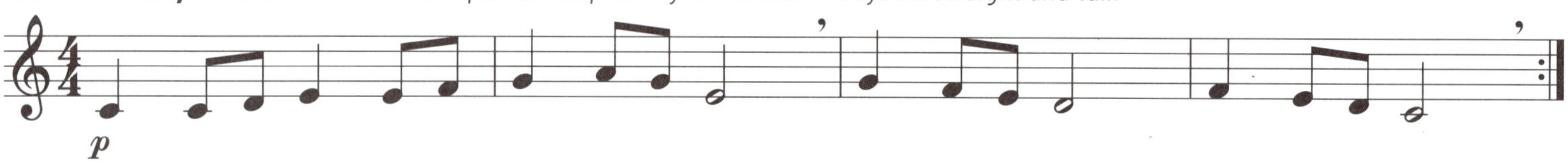


### 44. CANDY MOUNTAIN ROCK

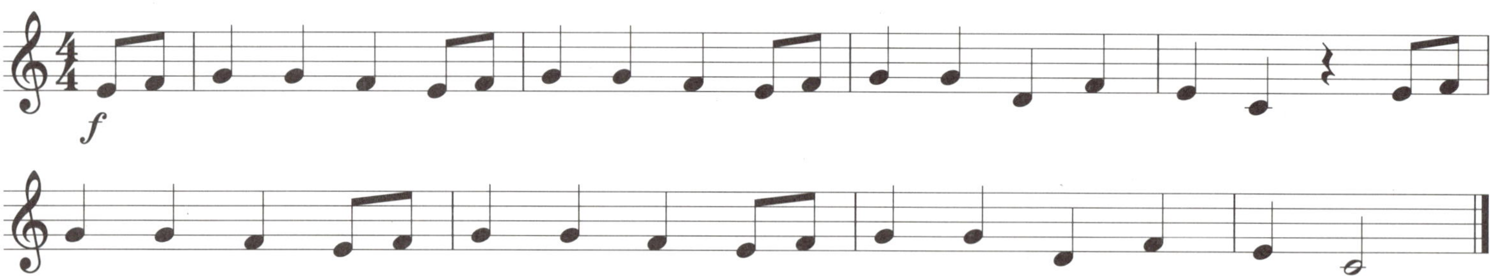


**HISTORY**

Italian composer **Gioachino Rossini** (1792–1868) began composing as a teenager and was very proficient on the piano, viola and horn. He wrote "William Tell" at age 37 as the last of his forty operas, and its familiar theme is still heard today on radio and television.

### 45. ESSENTIAL ELEMENTS QUIZ – WILLIAM TELL

Gioachino Rossini

## 2/4 Time Signature

= **2 beats** per measure
= **Quarter** note gets one beat

## Conducting

Practice conducting this two-beat pattern.

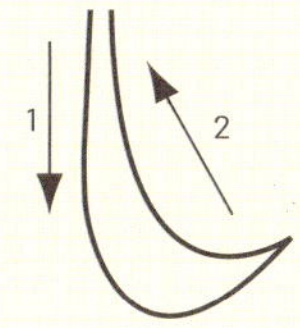


### 46. RHYTHM RAP

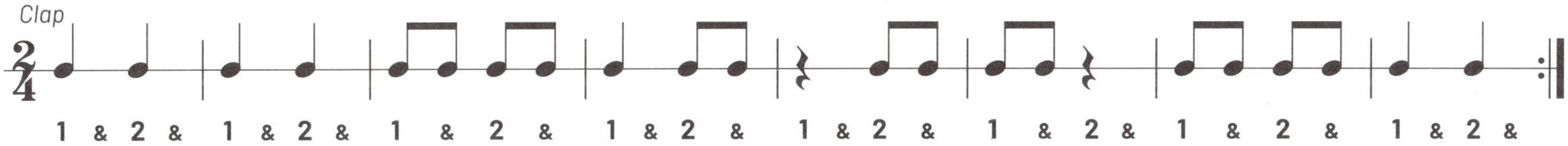


### 47. TWO BY TWO

## Tempo Markings

*Tempo* is the speed of music. Tempo markings are usually written above the staff, in Italian.
**Allegro** – Fast tempo  **Moderato** – Medium tempo  **Andante** – Slower walking tempo

### 48. HIGH SCHOOL CADETS – March

John Philip Sousa

Reproduced by Permission of Boosey & Hawkes Music Publishers Ltd.

### 49. HEY, HO! NOBODY'S HOME – New Note

## Dynamics

***Crescendo*** (gradually louder)  ***Decrescendo*** or ***Diminuendo*** (gradually softer)

### 50. CLAP THE DYNAMICS

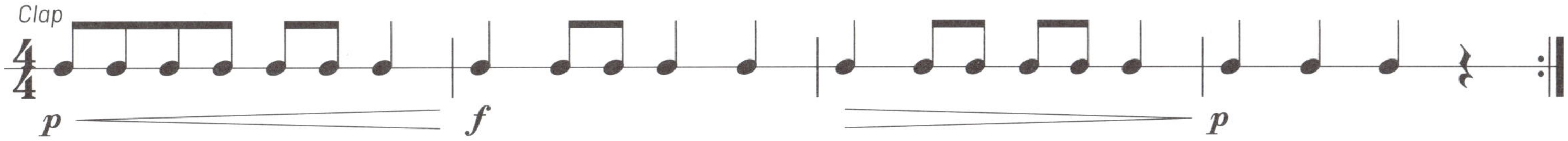


### 51. PLAY THE DYNAMICS

*Looking for some more fun music to play?*
*See the inside front cover for instructions on accessing recent popular Bonus Songs.*

# PERFORMANCE SPOTLIGHT

## 52. PERFORMANCE WARM-UPS

### TONE BUILDER

### RHYTHM ETUDE

### RHYTHM RAP

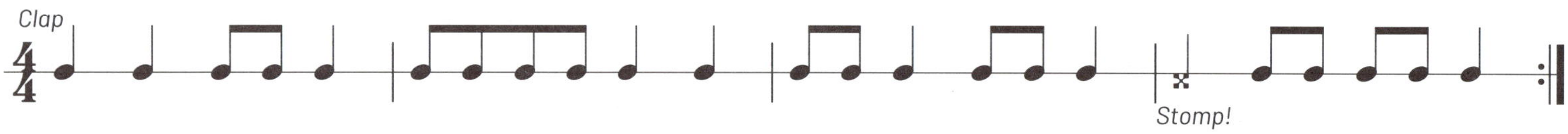


### CHORALE

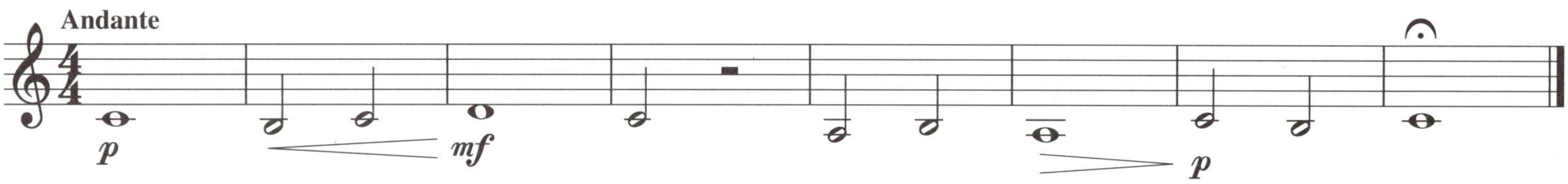


## 53. AURA LEE – Duet or Band Arrangement

*(Part A = Melody, Part B = Harmony)*

George R. Poulton

## 54. FRÈRE JACQUES – Round *(When group A reaches ②, group B begins at ①)*

French Folk Song

# PERFORMANCE SPOTLIGHT

## 55. WHEN THE SAINTS GO MARCHING IN – Band Arrangement

Arr. by John Higgins

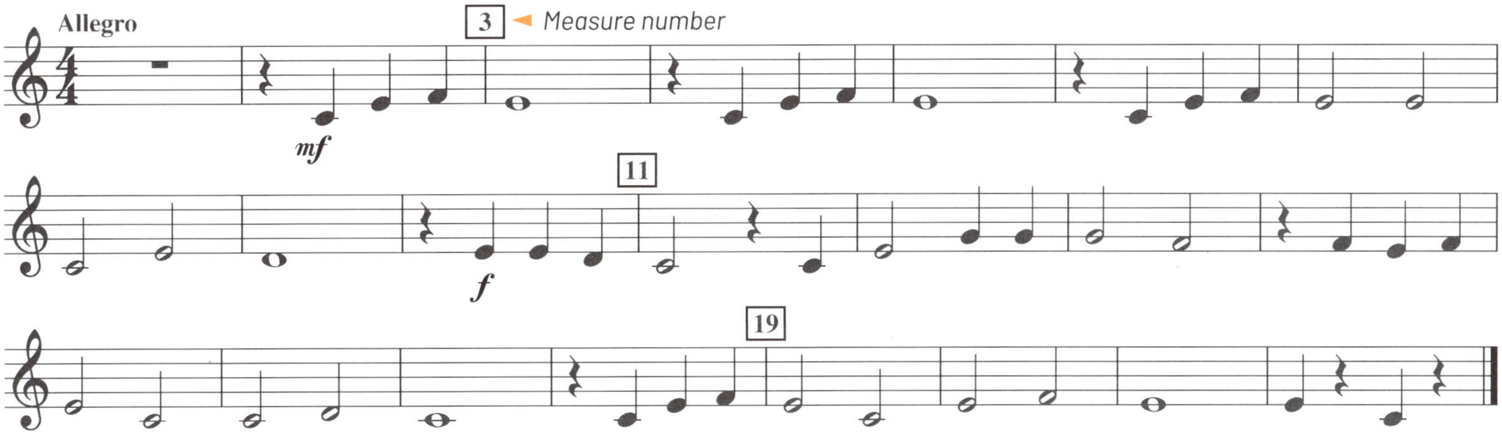


## 56. OLD MACDONALD HAD A BAND – Section Feature

## 57. ODE TO JOY (from Symphony No. 9)

Ludwig van Beethoven
Arr. by John Higgins

## 58. HARD ROCK BLUES – Encore

John Higgins

## Tie

A curved line connecting notes of the same pitch.
Play one note for the combined counts of the tied notes.

= 2 Beats

### 59. FIT TO BE TIED

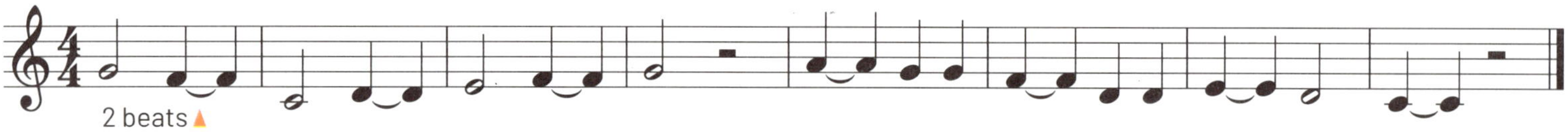


### 60. ALOUETTE

French-Canadian Folk Song

## Dotted Half Note

 = 3 Beats

1 & 2 & 3 &

 Dot

A dot adds half the value of the note.

2 beats + 1 beat = 3 beats

### 61. ALOUETTE – THE SEQUEL

French-Canadian Folk Song

### 62. IT'S RAINING

Allegro

### 63. NEW DIRECTIONS - New Note

**G**

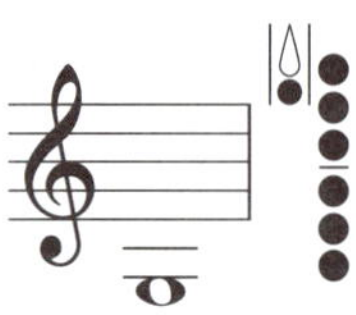

### 64. THE NOBLES

*Always use a full airstream. Keep fingers above the tone holes, curved naturally.*

### 65. ESSENTIAL ELEMENTS QUIZ

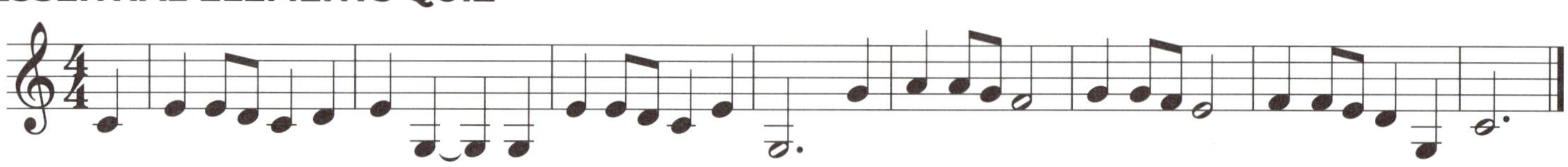

## $\frac{3}{4}$ Time Signature

= **3 beats** per measure
= **Quarter** note gets one beat

## Conducting

Practice conducting this three-beat pattern.

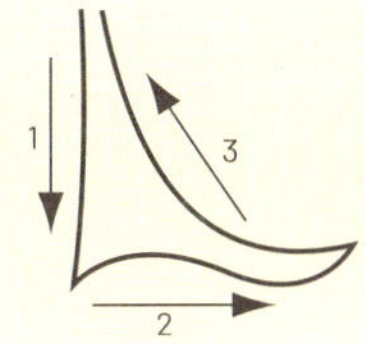


THEORY

### 66. RHYTHM RAP

### 67. THREE BEAT JAM

### 68. BARCAROLLE

Jacques Offenbach

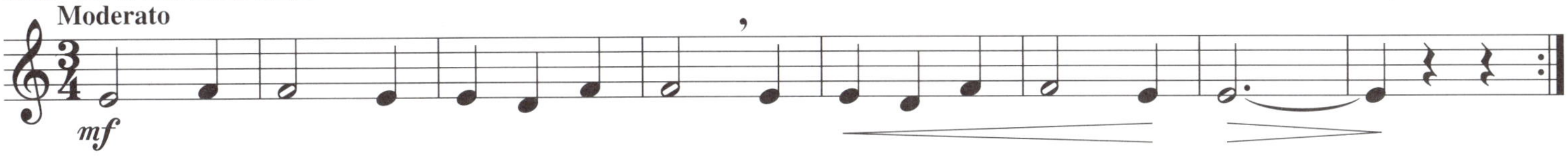


Norwegian composer **Edvard Grieg** (1843-1907) wrote *Peer Gynt Suite* for a play by Henrik Ibsen in 1875, the year before the telephone was invented by Alexander Graham Bell. "Morning" is a melody from *Peer Gynt Suite*. Music used in plays, or in films and television, is called **incidental music**.

HISTORY

### 69. MORNING (from Peer Gynt)

Edvard Grieg

## Accent

Emphasize the note.

### 70. ACCENT YOUR TALENT

**Latin American music** has its roots in the African, Native American, Spanish and Portuguese cultures. This diverse music features lively accompaniments by drums and other percussion instruments such as maracas and claves. Music from Latin America continues to influence jazz, classical and popular styles of music. "Chiapanecas" is a popular children's dance and game song.

HISTORY

### 71. MEXICAN CLAPPING SONG ("Chiapanecas")

Latin American Folk Song

### 72. ESSENTIAL CREATIVITY

*Compose your own music for measures 3 and 4 using this rhythm:*

THEORY

## Accidental

Any sharp, flat or natural sign which appears in the music without being in the key signature is called an **accidental**.

## Flat ♭

A **flat** sign lowers the pitch of a note by a half-step. The note B-flat sounds a half-step below B, and all B's become B-flats for the rest of the measure where they occur.

### 73. HOT MUFFINS – New Note

### 74. COSSACK DANCE

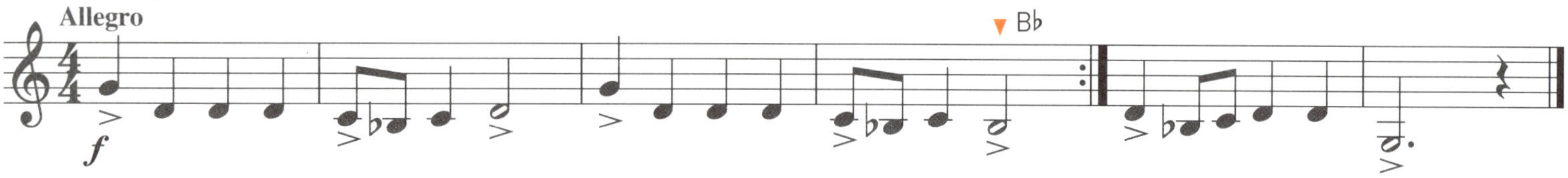


### 75. BASIC BLUES – New Note

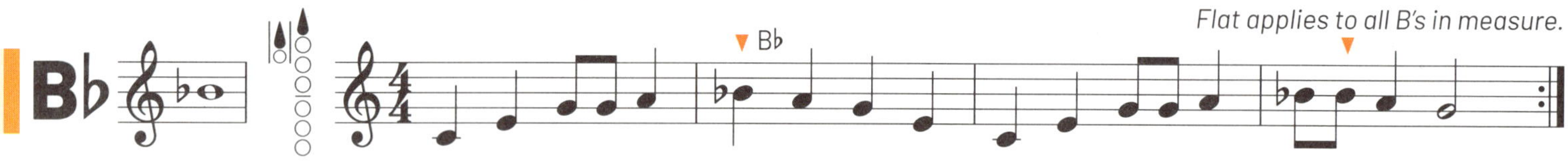


THEORY

## New Key Signature

This Key Signature indicates the *Key of F* – play all B's as B-flats.

## 1st & 2nd Endings

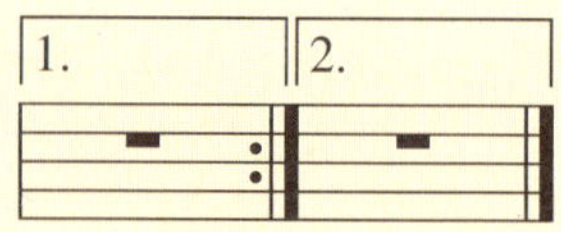


Play through the 1st Ending. Then play the repeated section of music, **skipping** the 1st Ending and playing the 2nd Ending.

### 76. HIGH FLYING

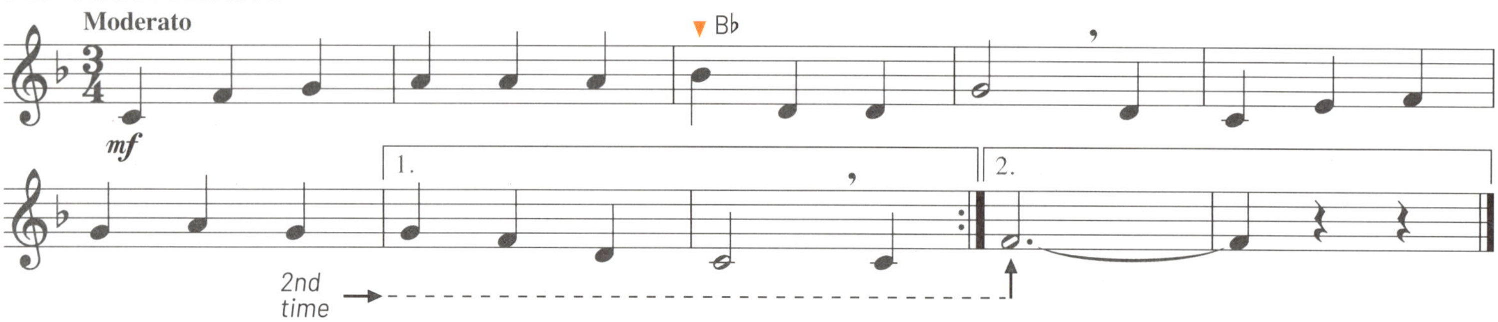


HISTORY

**Japanese folk music** actually has its origins in ancient China. "Sakura, Sakura" was performed on instruments such as the **koto**, a 13-string instrument that is more than 4000 years old, and the **shakuhachi** or bamboo flute. The unique sound of this ancient Japanese melody results from the pentatonic (or five-note) sequence used in this tonal system.

### 77. SAKURA, SAKURA – Band Arrangement

Japanese Folk Song
Arr. by John Higgins

## 78. UP ON A HOUSETOP

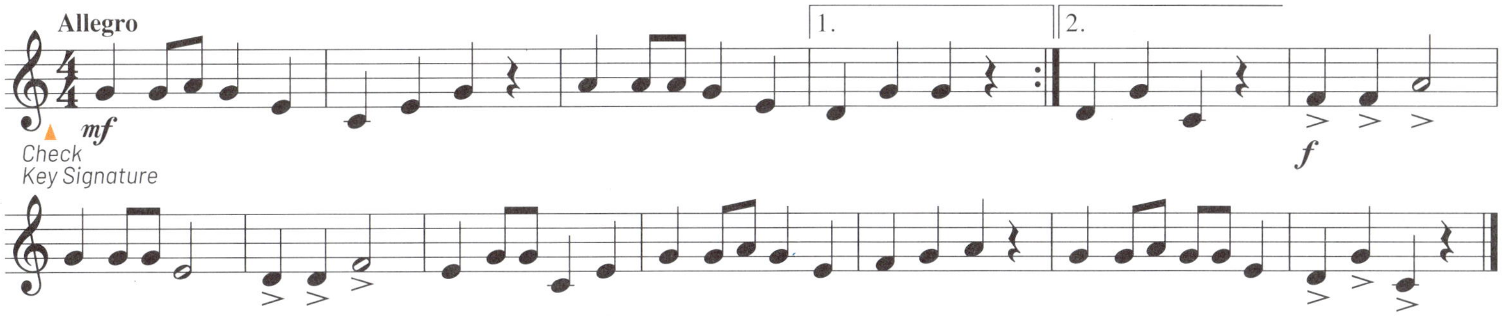


## 79. JOLLY OLD ST. NICK – Duet

*See page 9 for additional holiday music, MY DREYDL and JINGLE BELLS.*

## 80. THE BIG AIRSTREAM

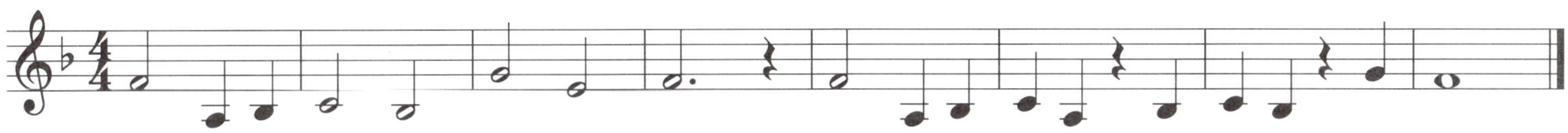

## 81. WALTZ THEME (THE MERRY WIDOW WALTZ)

Franz Lehar

© Glocken Verlag Ltd., London
Reproduced by Permission

## 82. AIR TIME – New Note

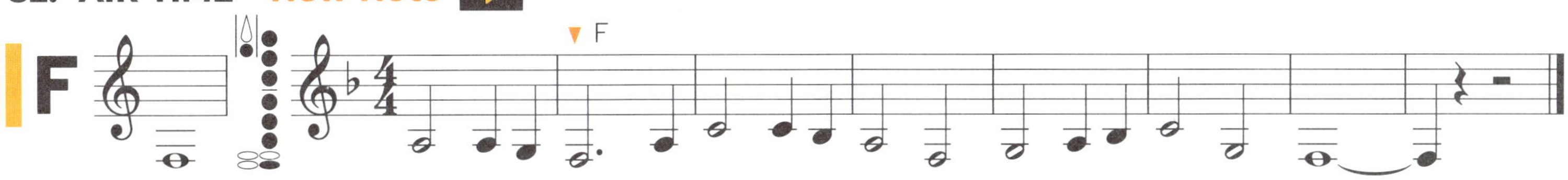


## 83. DOWN BY THE STATION

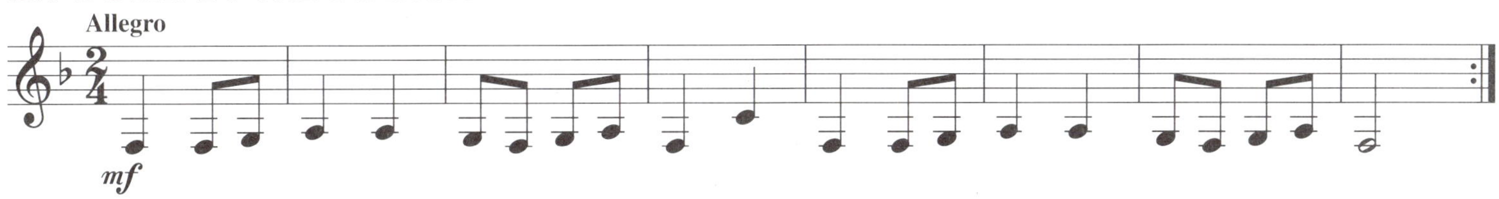


## 84. ESSENTIAL ELEMENTS QUIZ

## 85. ESSENTIAL CREATIVITY *Using these notes, improvise your own rhythms:*

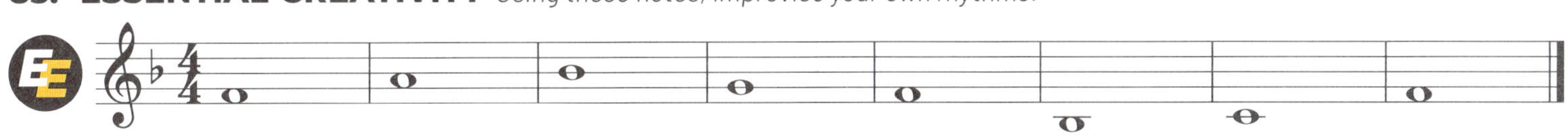

# DAILY WARM-UPS

WORK-OUTS FOR TONE & TECHNIQUE

## 86. TONE BUILDER *Use a steady stream of air.*

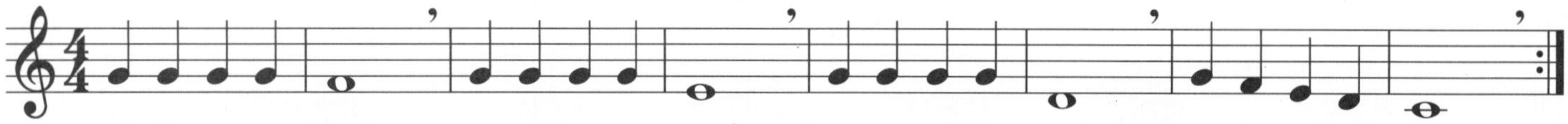

## 87. RHYTHM BUILDER

## 88. TECHNIQUE TRAX

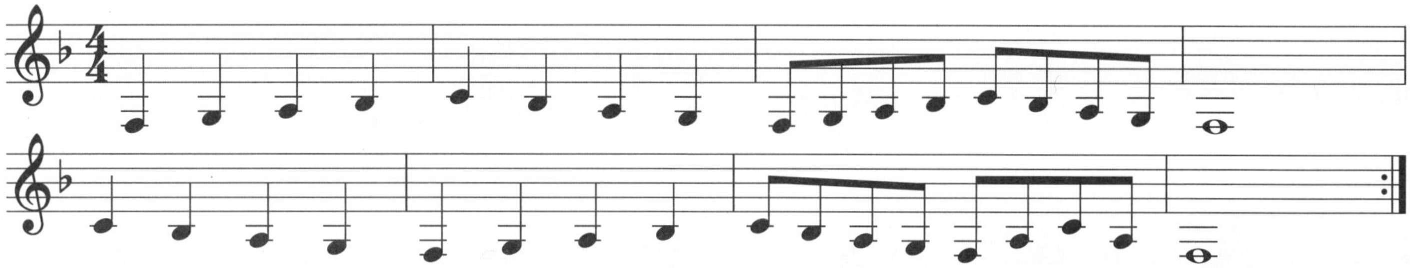

## 89. CHORALE *(Adapted from Cantata 147)*

Johann Sebastian Bach

THEORY

## Theme and Variations

A musical form featuring a **theme**, or primary melody, followed by **variations**, or altered versions of the theme.

## 90. VARIATIONS ON A FAMILIAR THEME

## D.C. al Fine

At the **D.C. al Fine** play again from the beginning, stopping at **Fine** *(fee'- nay)*. **D.C.** is the abbreviation for **Da Capo**, or "to the beginning," and **Fine** means "the end."

## 91. BANANA BOAT SONG

Caribbean Folk Song

## Sharp ♯

THEORY

A **sharp** sign raises the pitch of a note by a half-step. The note F-sharp sounds a half-step above F, and all F's become F-sharps for the rest of the measure where they occur.

### 92. RAZOR'S EDGE – New Note

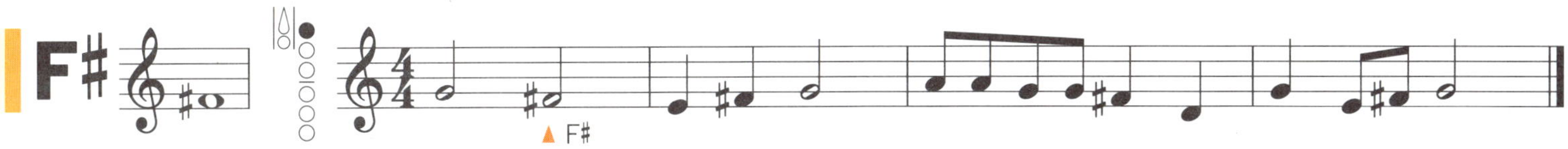


### 93. THE MUSIC BOX

HISTORY

**African-American spirituals** originated in the 1700's, midway through the period of slavery in the United States. One of the largest categories of true American folk music, these primarily religious songs were sung and passed on for generations without being written down. The first collection of spirituals was published in 1867, four years after The Emancipation Proclamation was signed into law.

### 94. EZEKIEL SAW THE WHEEL

African-American Spiritual

**Slur**

A curved line which connects notes of different pitch. Tongue only the first note in a **slur**.

### 95. SMOOTH OPERATOR

### 96. GLIDING ALONG

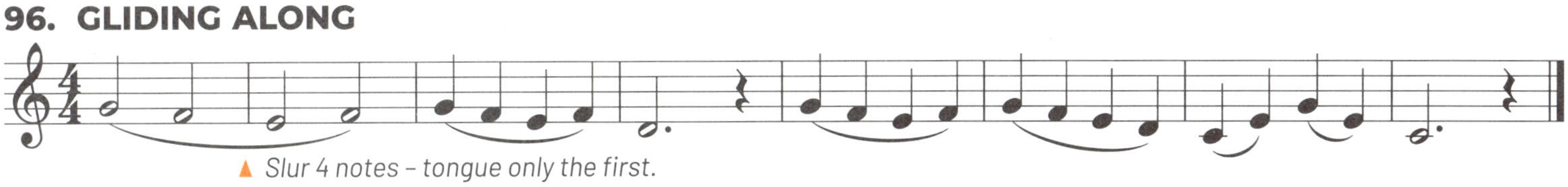


HISTORY

**Ragtime** is an American music style that was popular from the 1890's until the time of World War I. This early form of jazz brought fame to pianists like "Jelly Roll" Morton and Scott Joplin, who wrote "The Entertainer" and "Maple Leaf Rag." Surprisingly, the style was incorporated into some orchestral music by Igor Stravinsky and Claude Debussy. The trombones now learn to play a *glissando*, a technique used in ragtime and other styles of music.

### 97. TROMBONE RAG

### 98. ESSENTIAL ELEMENTS QUIZ

## 99. TAKE THE LEAD *Always cover the tone holes completely.*

**THEORY**

**Phrase** A musical "sentence" which is often 2 or 4 measures long. Try to play a **phrase** in one breath.

## 100. THE COLD WIND

## 101. PHRASEOLOGY *Write in the breath mark(s) between the phrases.*

**THEORY**

**New Key Signature**

This **Key Signature** indicates the *Key of G* – play all F's as F-sharps.

**Multiple Measure Rest**

The number above the staff tells you how many full measures to rest.
Count each measure of rest in sequence: **1**-2-3-4 **2**-2-3-4

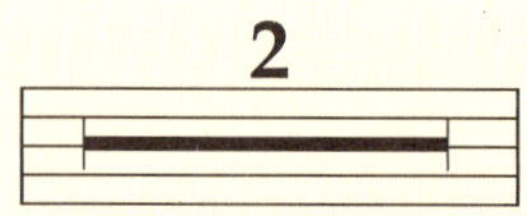


## 102. SATIN LATIN

**HISTORY**

German composer **Johann Sebastian Bach** (1685–1750) was part of a large family of famous musicians and became the most recognized composer of the Baroque era. Beginning as a choir member, Bach soon became an organist, a teacher, and a prolific composer, writing more than 600 masterworks. This *Minuet*, or dance in 3/4 time, was written as a teaching piece for use with an early form of the piano.

## 103. MINUET – Duet

Johann Sebastian Bach

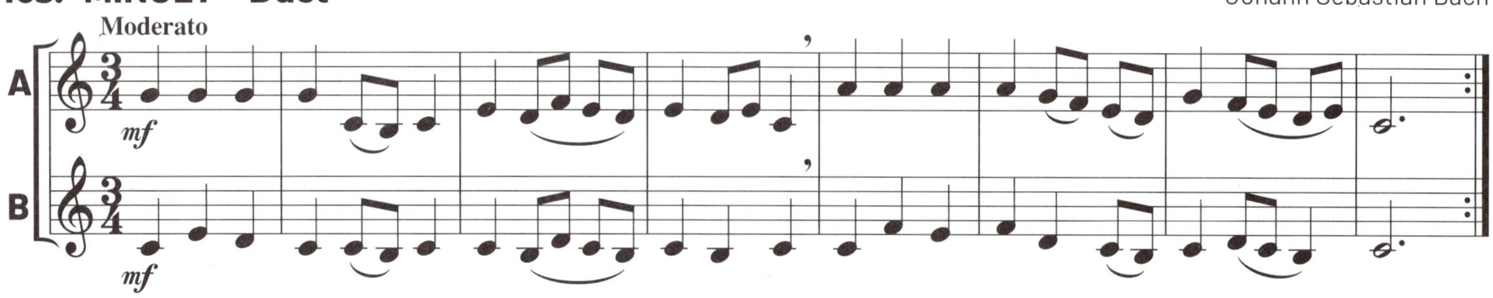


## 104. ESSENTIAL CREATIVITY *This melody can be played in 3/4 or 4/4. Pencil in either time signature, draw the bar lines and play. Now erase the bar lines and try the other time signature. Do the phrases sound different?*

THEORY

## Natural ♮

A **natural** sign cancels a flat (♭) or sharp (♯) and remains in effect for the entire measure.

### 105. NATURALLY

HISTORY

Austrian composer **Franz Peter Schubert** (1797-1828) lived a shorter life than any other great composer, but he created an incredible amount of music: more than 600 art-songs (concert music for voice and accompaniment), ten symphonies, chamber music, operas, choral works and piano pieces. His "March Militaire" was originally a piano duet.

### 106. MARCH MILITAIRE

Franz Schubert

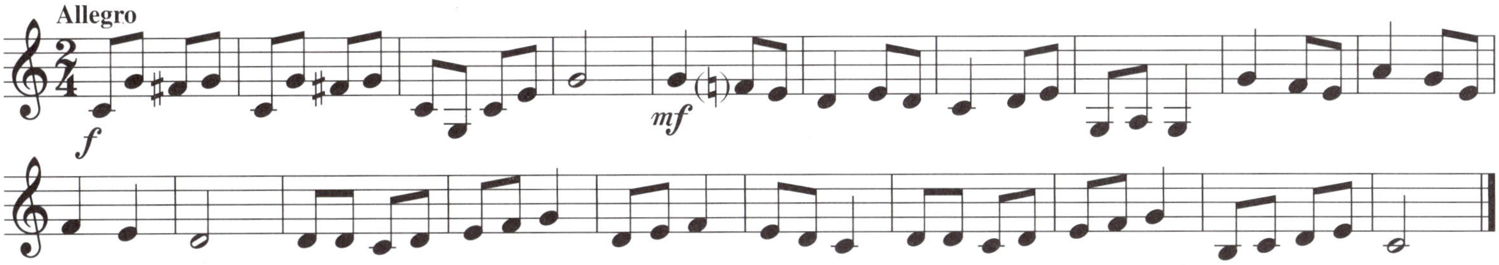


### 107. THE FLAT ZONE – New Note

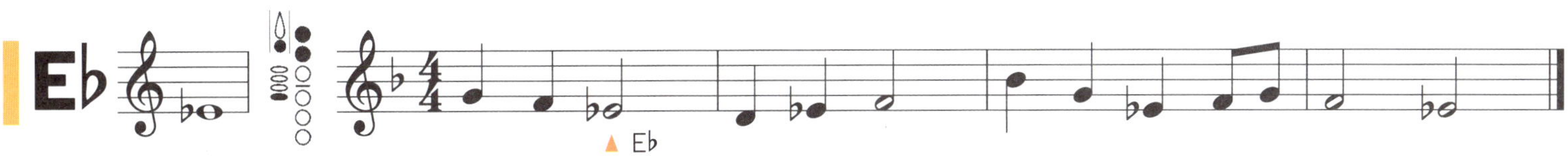


### 108. ON TOP OF OLD SMOKEY

American Folk Song

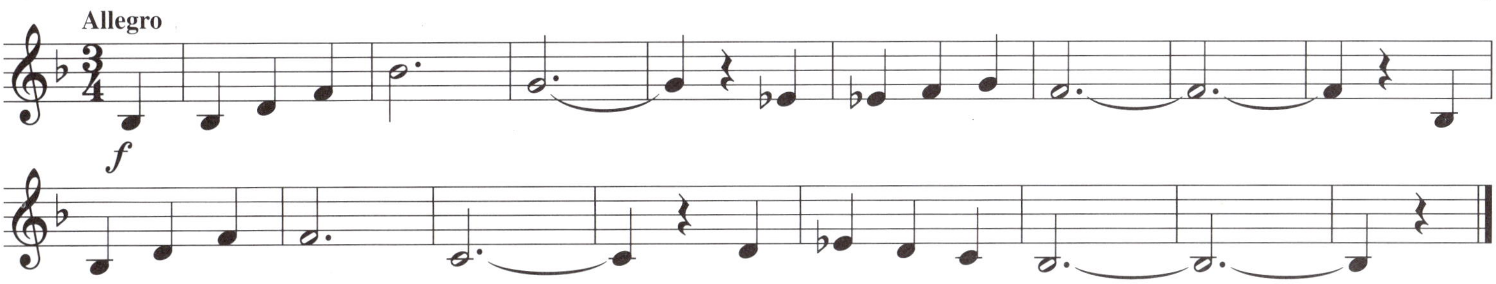


HISTORY

**Boogie-woogie** is a style of the **blues**, and it was first recorded by pianist Clarence "Pine Top" Smith in 1928, one year after Charles Lindbergh's solo flight across the Atlantic. A form of jazz, blues music features altered notes and is usually written in 12-measure verses, like "Bottom Bass Boogie."

### 109. BOTTOM BASS BOOGIE – Duet

## Dotted Quarter & Eighth Notes

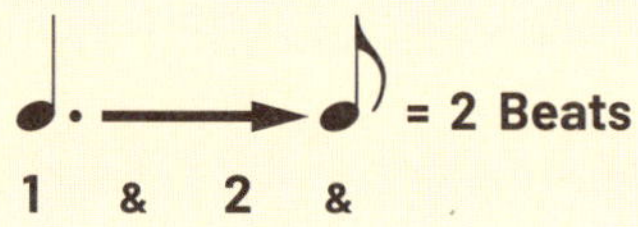


A **dot** adds half the value of the quarter note.

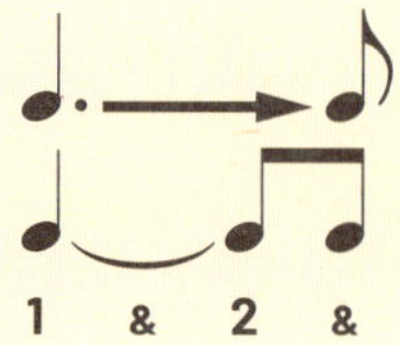

A single **eighth note** has a **flag** on the stem.

### 110. RHYTHM RAP

### 111. THE DOT ALWAYS COUNTS

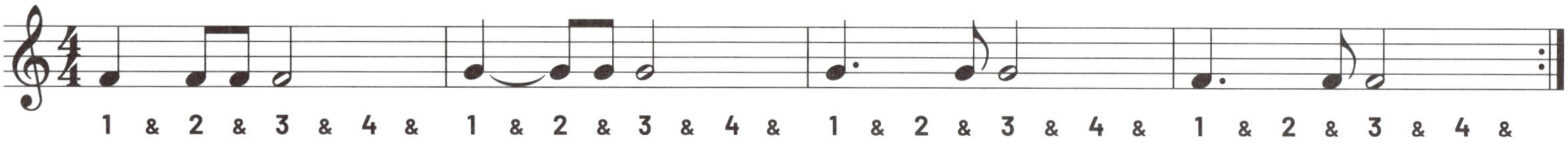


### 112. ALL THROUGH THE NIGHT

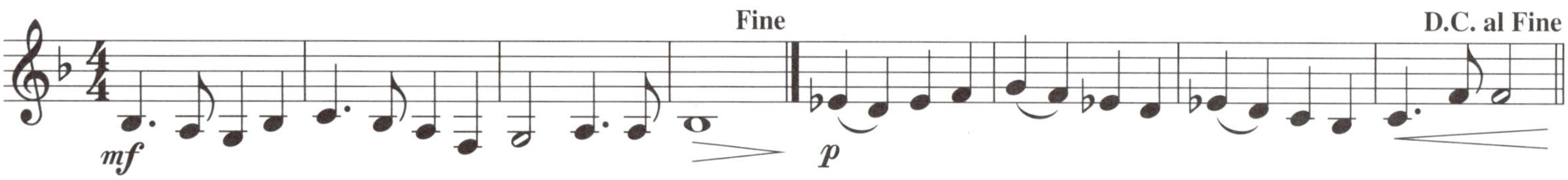


### 113. SEA CHANTY *Always use a full airstream.*

English Folk Song

### 114. SCARBOROUGH FAIR

English Folk Song

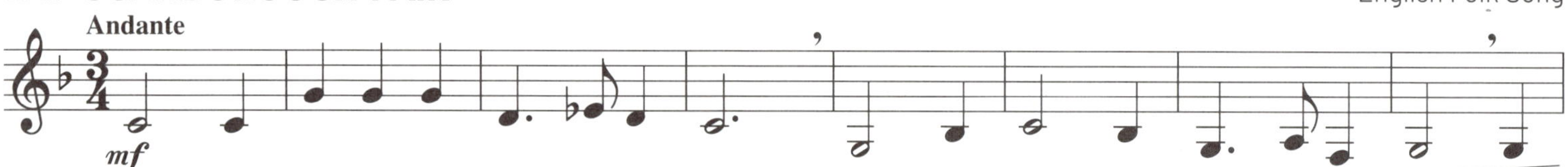

### 115. RHYTHM RAP

### 116. THE TURNAROUND

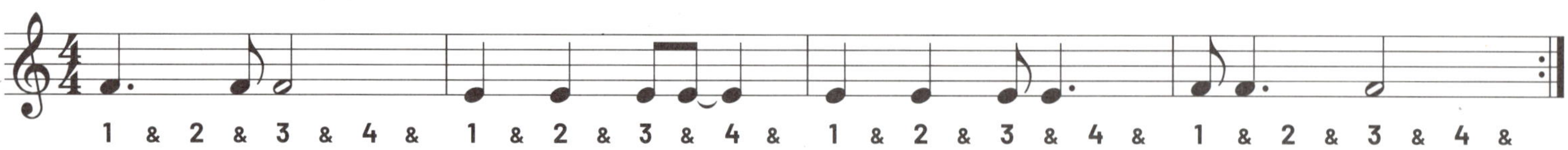


### 117. ESSENTIAL ELEMENTS QUIZ – AULD LANG SYNE

Scottish Folk Song

# PERFORMANCE SPOTLIGHT

## Solo with Piano Accompaniment

You can perform this solo with or without a piano accompanist. Play it for the band, the school or your family. It is part of **Symphony No. 9 ("From The New World")** by Czech composer **Antonin Dvorák** (1841–1904). He wrote it while visiting America in 1893, and was inspired to include melodies from American folksongs and spirituals. This is the **Largo** (or "very slow tempo") theme.

### 118. THEME FROM "NEW WORLD SYMPHONY"

Antonin Dvorák

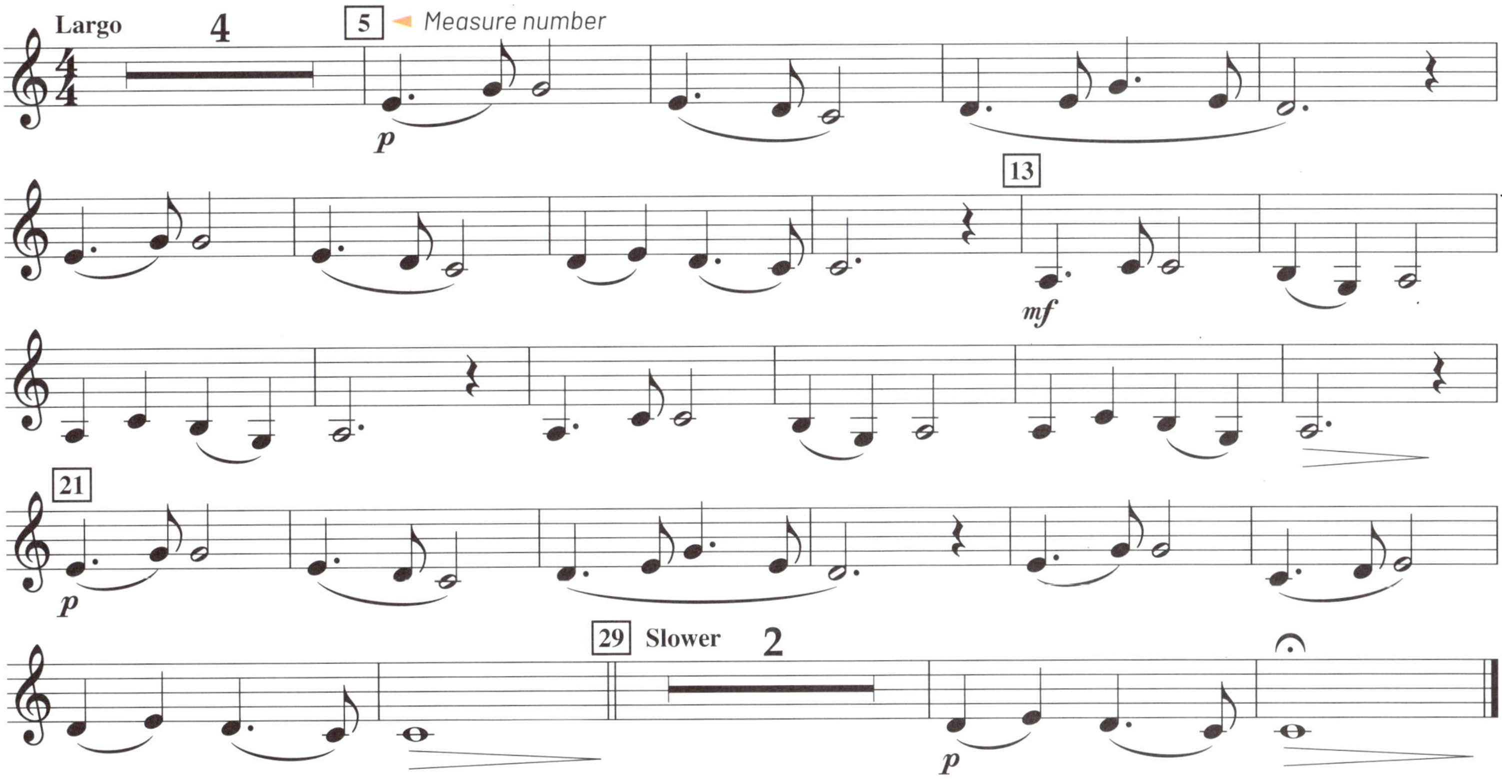


Piano Accompaniment

## SPECIAL CLARINET TECHNIQUE – Register Key

Notes above B♭ require the **Register Key** and are called "upper register" notes.

Remember the following:

1. Maintain a steady, fast stream of air.
2. Keep your embouchure firm and your chin flat.
3. Roll your thumb up slightly to open the register key.

*Great musicians give encouragement to fellow performers. On this page, clarinetists learn their instruments' upper register in the "Grenadilla Gorilla Jumps" (named after the grenadilla wood used to make clarinets). Brass players learn lip slurs, a new warm-up pattern. The success of your band depends on everyone's effort and encouragement.*

### 119. GRENADILLA GORILLA JUMP No. 1

### 120. JUMPIN' UP AND DOWN

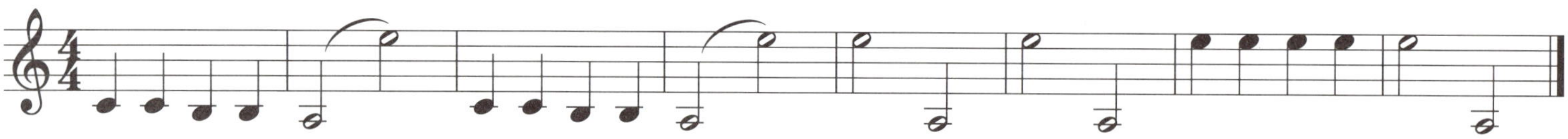

### 121. GRENADILLA GORILLA JUMP No. 2

### 122. JUMPIN' FOR JOY

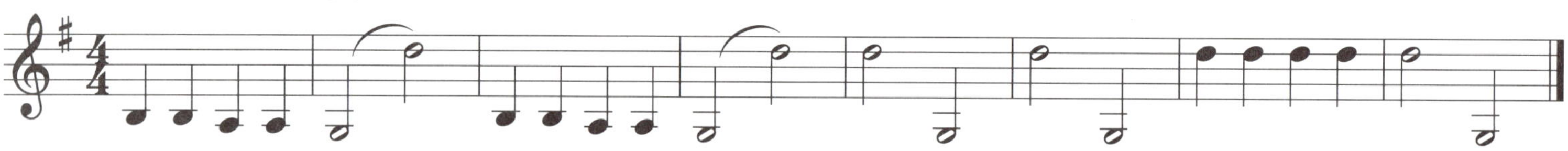

### 123. GRENADILLA GORILLA JUMP No. 3

### 124. JUMPIN' JACKS

THEORY

## Interval

The distance between two pitches is an **interval**. Starting with "1" on the lower note, count each line and space between the notes. The number of the higher note is the distance of the interval.

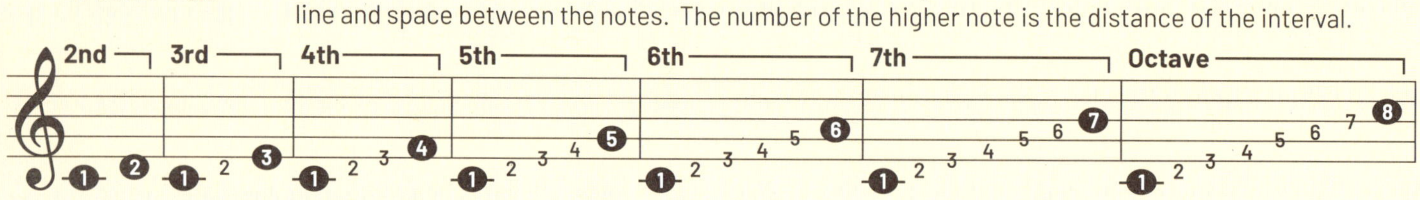


### 125. ESSENTIAL ELEMENTS QUIZ

*Write in the numbers of the intervals, counting up from the lower notes.*

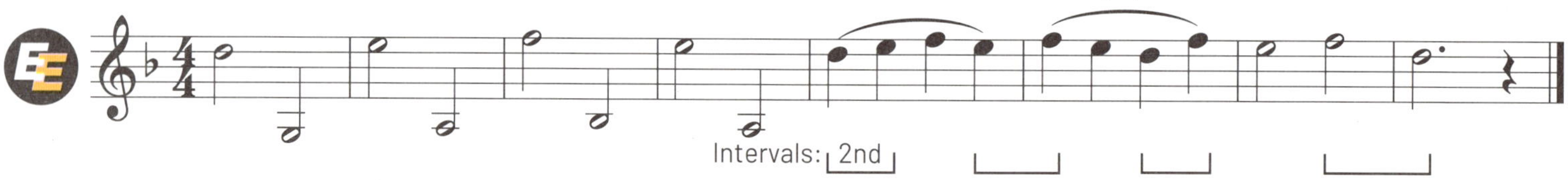


***Additional bonus songs are available online. See the inside front cover for details.***

### 126. GRENADILLA GORILLA JUMP No. 4

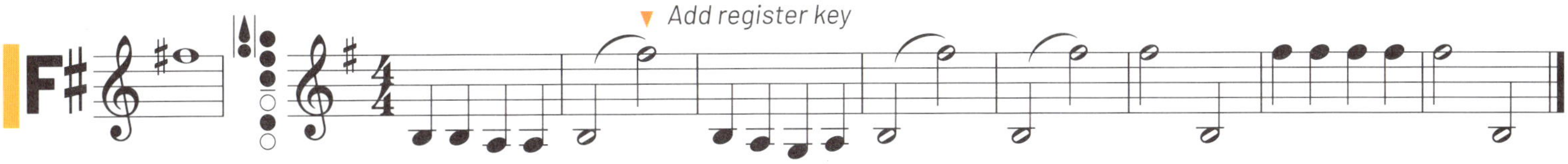


### 127. THREE IS THE COUNT

### 128. GRENADILLA GORILLA JUMP No. 5

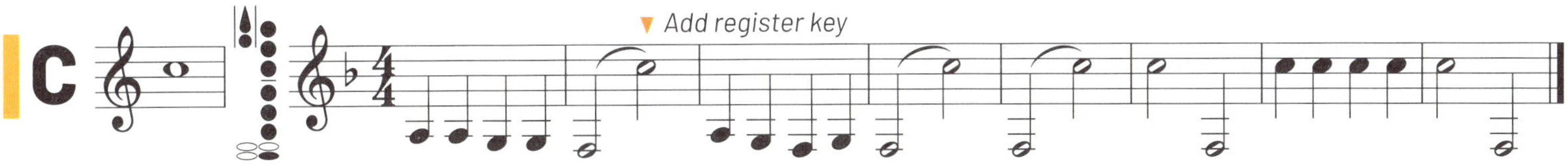


### 129. TECHNIQUE TRAX

**Crossing the Break** *When alternating between high and low registers, you can keep your* ***right hand fingers down*** *on G, A and B♭:*

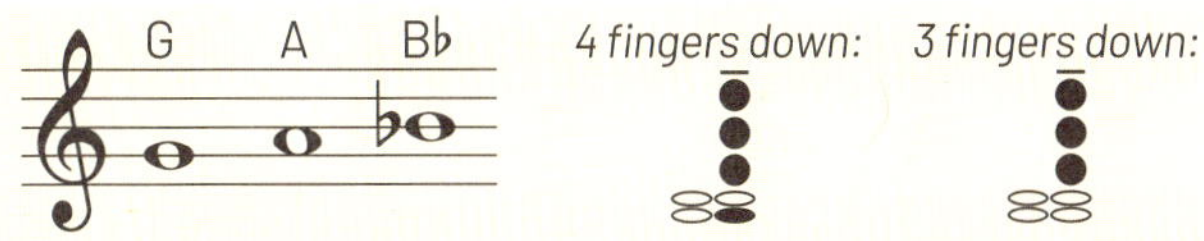


### 130. CROSSING OVER

**Trio** A **trio** is a composition with three parts played together. Practice this trio with two other players and listen for 3-part harmony.

### 131. KUM BAH YAH – Trio *Always check the key signature.*

African Folk Song

## Repeat Signs

Repeat the section of music enclosed by the **repeat signs**. *(If 1st and 2nd endings are used, they are played as usual – but go back only to the first repeat sign, not to the beginning.)*

### 132. MICHAEL ROW THE BOAT ASHORE

African-American Spiritual

### 133. AUSTRIAN WALTZ

Austrian Folk Song

### 134. BOTANY BAY

Australian Folk Song

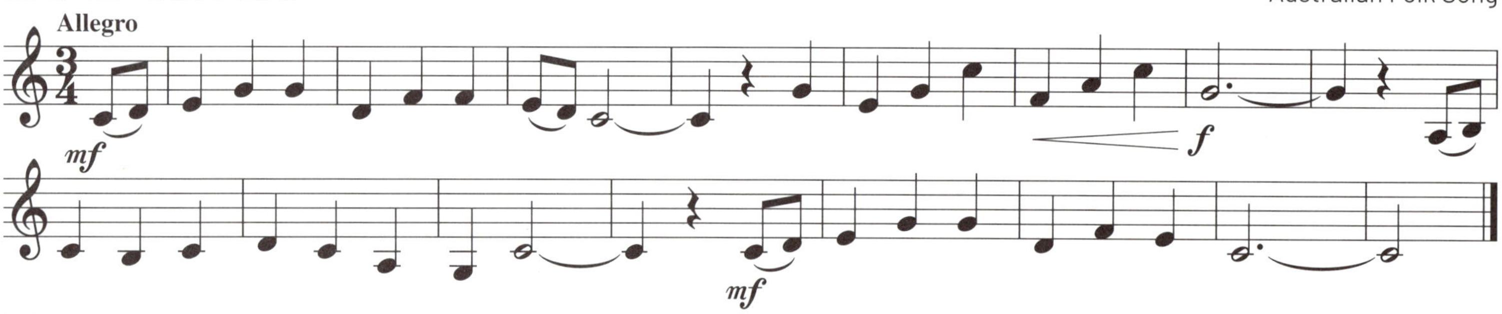


THEORY

## C Time Signature

= **Common Time**
(Same as $\frac{4}{4}$)

## Conducting

Practice conducting this four-beat pattern.

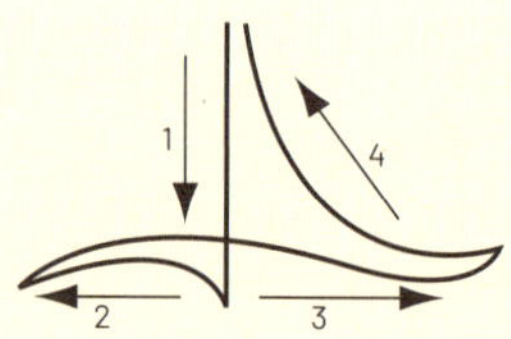


### 135. TECHNIQUE TRAX *Practice at all dynamic levels.*

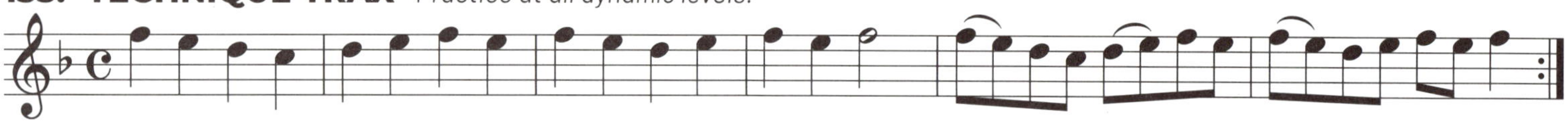

### 136. FINLANDIA

Jean Sibelius

© Breitkopf & Haertel, Wiesbaden - Leipzig

### 137. ESSENTIAL CREATIVITY

*Create your own variations by penciling in a dot and a flag to change the rhythm of any measure from* 

**138. EASY GORILLA JUMPS** *On this exercise, clarinets play a special part.*

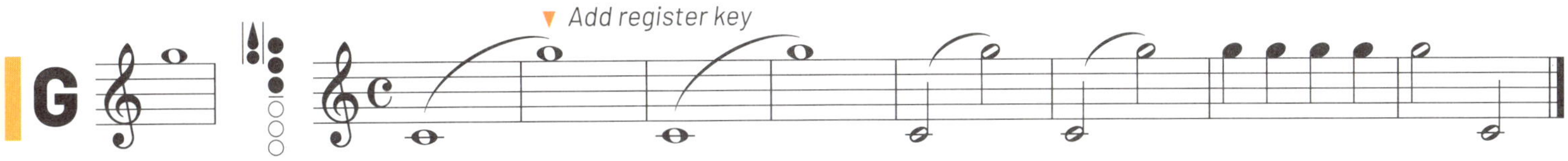


**139. TECHNIQUE TRAX** *Always check the key signature.*

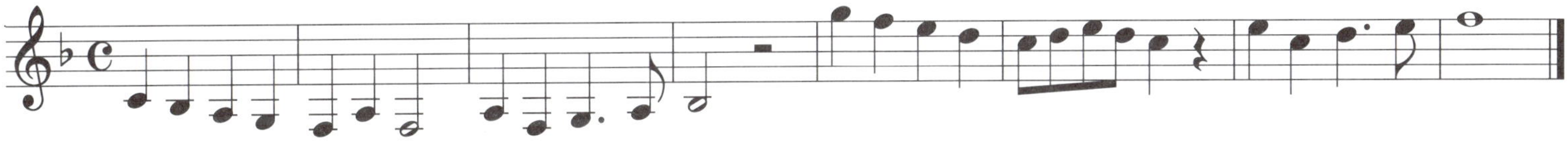

**140. MORE TECHNIQUE TRAX**

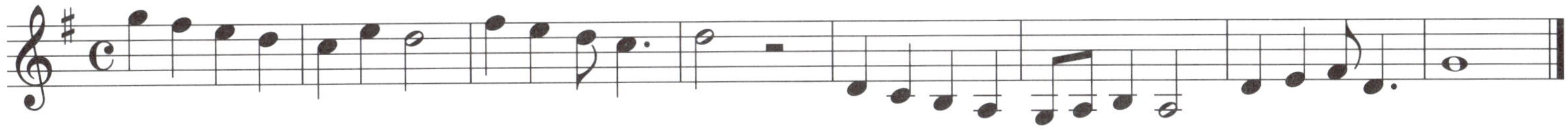

**141. GERMAN FOLK SONG**

**142. THE SAINTS GO MARCHIN' AGAIN** James Black and Katherine Purvis

**143. LOWLAND GORILLA WALK** *Be sure the pads of your fingers cover the holes completely.*

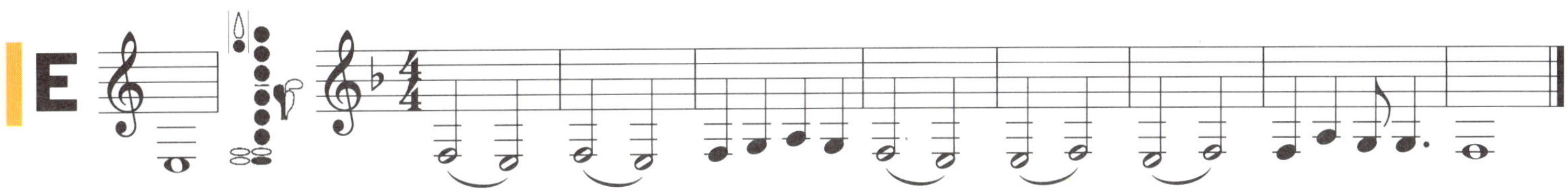


**144. SMOOTH SAILING**

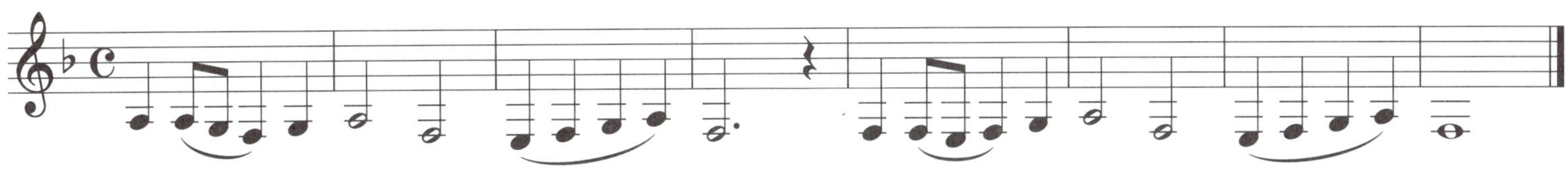

**145. MORE GORILLA JUMPS** *On this exercise, clarinets play a special part.*

**146. FULL COVERAGE** *Be sure to cover the holes completely.*

THEORY

## Scale

A **scale** is a sequence of notes in ascending or descending order. Like a musical "ladder," each step is the next consecutive note in the key. This scale is in your Key of C (no sharps or flats), so the top and bottom notes are both C's. The interval between the C's is an octave.

### 147. CONCERT B♭ SCALE (Clarinet – C SCALE)

THEORY

## Chord & Arpeggio

When two or more notes are played together, they form a **chord** or **harmony**. This C chord is built from the 1st, 3rd and 5th steps of the C scale. The 8th step is the same as the 1st, but it is an octave higher. An **arpeggio** is a "broken" chord whose notes are played individually.

### 148. IN HARMONY *Divide the notes of the chords between band members and play together. Does the arpeggio sound like a chord?*

### 149. SCALE AND ARPEGGIO

HISTORY

Austrian composer **Franz Josef Haydn** (1732–1809) wrote 104 symphonies. Many of these works had nicknames and included brilliant, unique effects for their time. His *Symphony No. 94* was named "The Surprise Symphony" because the soft second movement included a sudden loud dynamic, intended to wake up an often sleepy audience. Pay special attention to dynamics when you play this famous theme.

### 150. THEME FROM "SURPRISE SYMPHONY"

Franz Josef Haydn

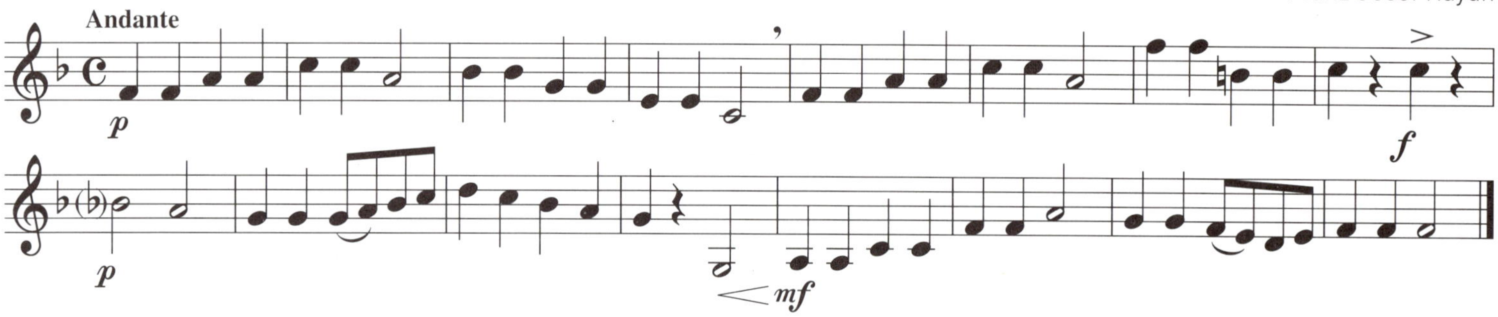


### 151. ESSENTIAL ELEMENTS QUIZ – THE STREETS OF LAREDO

American Folk Song

*Write in the note names before you play.*

# PERFORMANCE SPOTLIGHT

## 152. SCHOOL SPIRIT – Band Arrangement

W.T. Purdy
Arr. by John Higgins

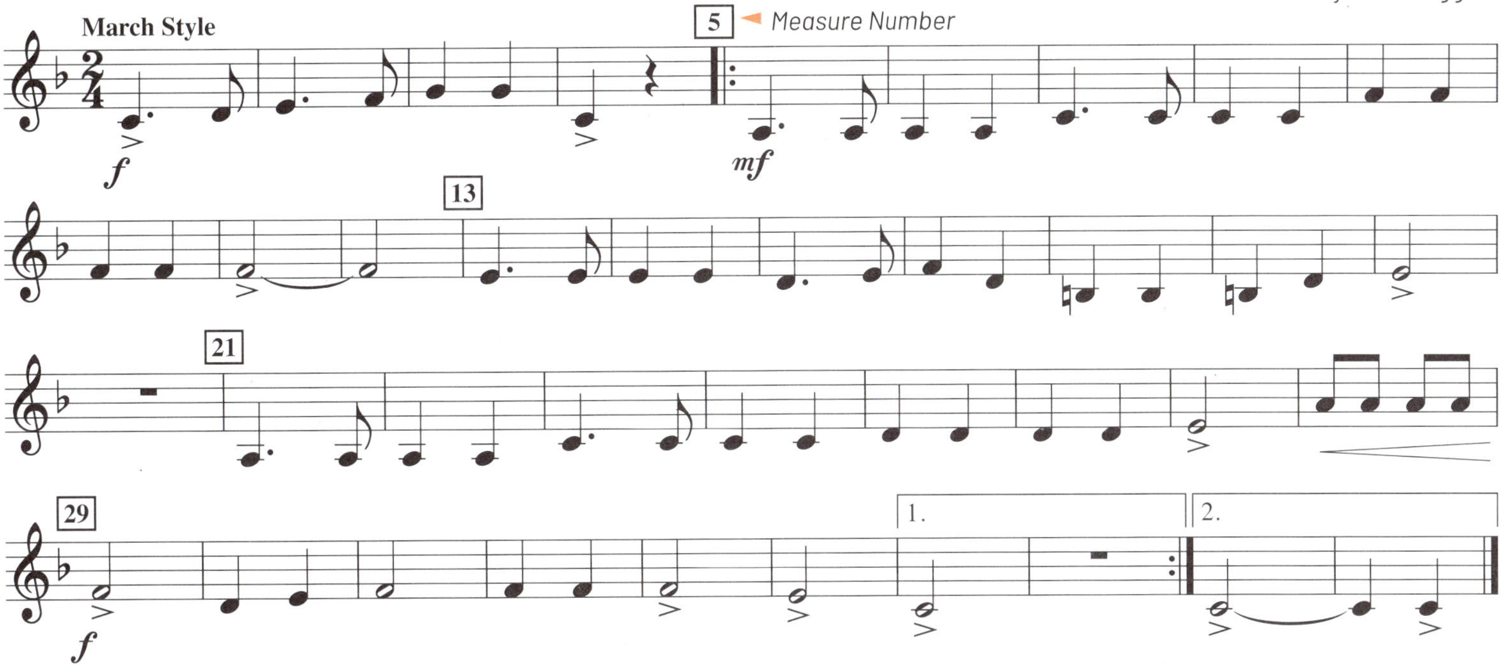


## Soli

When playing music marked **Soli**, you are part of a group "solo" or group feature. Listen carefully in "Carnival of Venice," and name the instruments that play the Soli part at each indicated measure number.

## 153. CARNIVAL OF VENICE – Band Arrangement

Julius Benedict
Arr. by John Higgins

# DAILY WARM-UPS

*WORK-OUTS FOR TONE & TECHNIQUE*

## 154. RANGE AND FLEXIBILITY BUILDER

## 155. TECHNIQUE TRAX

## 156. CHORALE

Johann Sebastian Bach

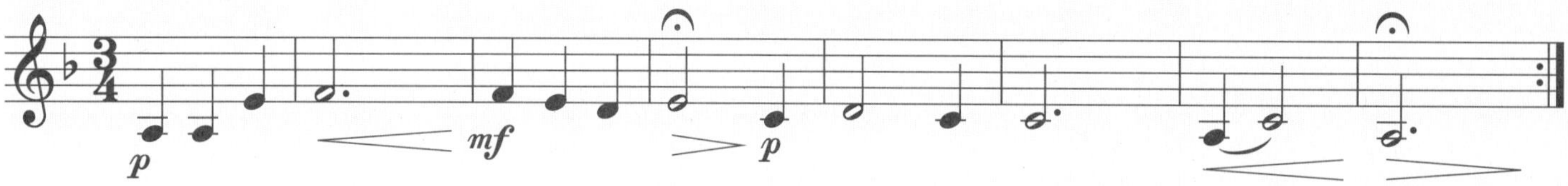


**HISTORY**

The traditional Hebrew melody "Hatikvah" has been Israel's national anthem since the nation's inception. At the Declaration of State in 1948, it was sung by the gathered assembly during the opening ceremony and played by members of the Palestine Symphony Orchestra at its conclusion.

## 157. HATIKVAH

Israeli National Anthem

## Eighth Note & Eighth Rest

♪ = 1/2 beat of sound

𝄾 = 1/2 beat of silence

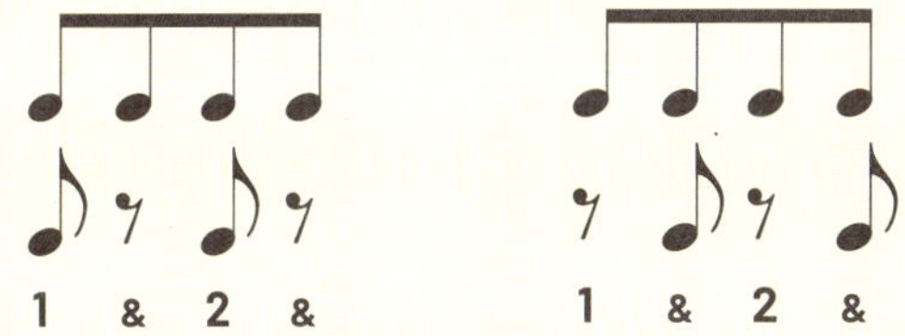


### 158. RHYTHM RAP

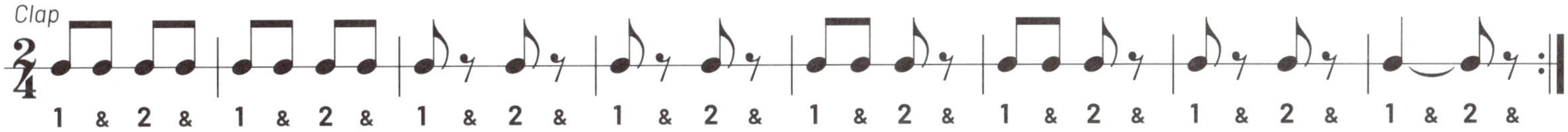


### 159. EIGHTH NOTE MARCH

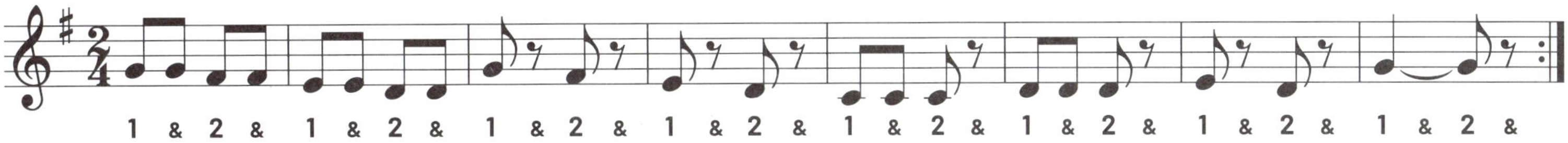


### 160. MINUET

Johann Sebastian Bach

### 161. RHYTHM RAP

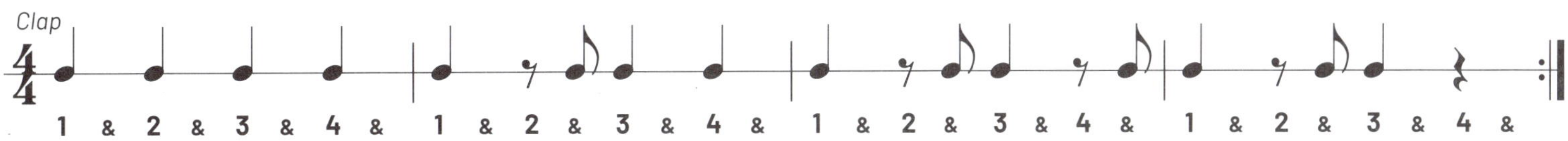


### 162. EIGHTH NOTES OFF THE BEAT

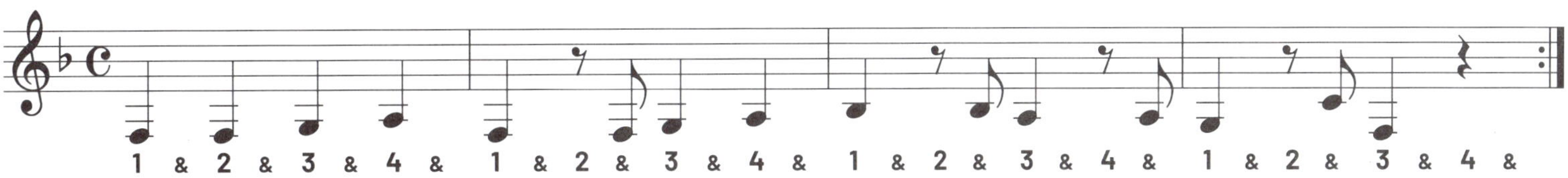


### 163. EIGHTH NOTE SCRAMBLE

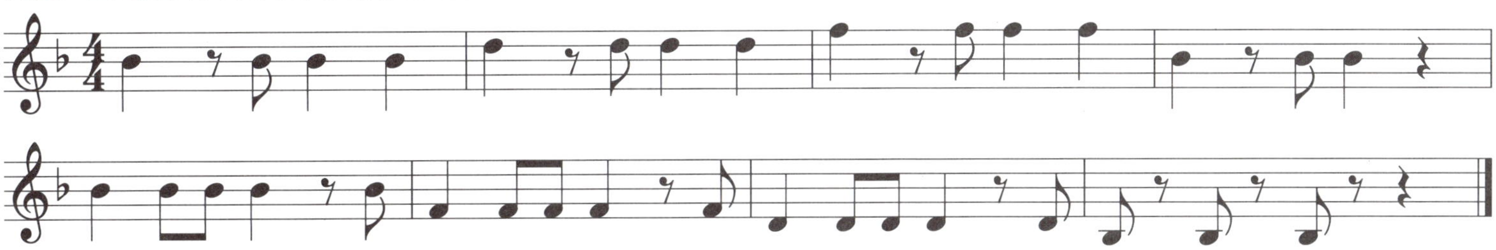

### 164. ESSENTIAL ELEMENTS QUIZ

## 165. DANCING MELODY – New Note

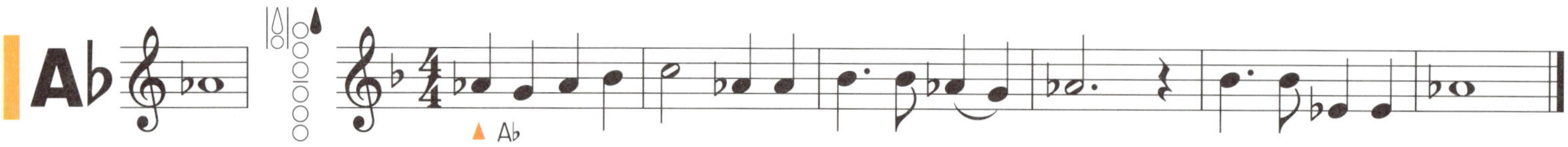


**HISTORY**

American composer and conductor **John Philip Sousa** (1854–1932) wrote 136 marches. Known as "The March King," Sousa wrote *The Stars And Stripes Forever*, *Semper Fidelis*, *The Washington Post* and many other patriotic works. Sousa's band performed all over the country, and his fame helped boost the popularity of bands in America. Here is a melody from his famous *El Capitan* operetta and march.

## 166. EL CAPITAN

John Philip Sousa

Reproduced by Permission of Boosey & Hawkes Music Publishers Ltd.

**HISTORY**

"O Canada," formerly known as the "National Song," was first performed during 1880 in French Canada. Robert Stanley Weir translated the English language version in 1908, but it was not adopted as the national anthem of Canada until 1980, one hundred years after its premiere.

## 167. O CANADA

Calixa Lavallee,
l'Hon. Judge Routhier and Justice R.S. Weir

## 168. ESSENTIAL ELEMENTS QUIZ – METER MANIA *Count and clap before playing. Can you conduct this?*

THEORY

## Enharmonics

Two notes that are written differently, but sound the same (and played with the same fingering) are called **enharmonics**. Your fingering chart on pages 46–47 shows the fingerings for the enharmonic notes on your instrument.

*On a piano keyboard, each black key is both a flat and a sharp:*

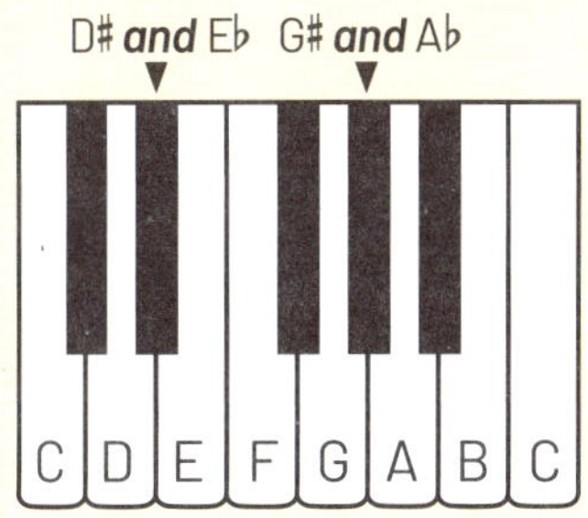


### 169. SNAKE CHARMER

*Enharmonic notes use the same fingering.*

**A♭/G♯**

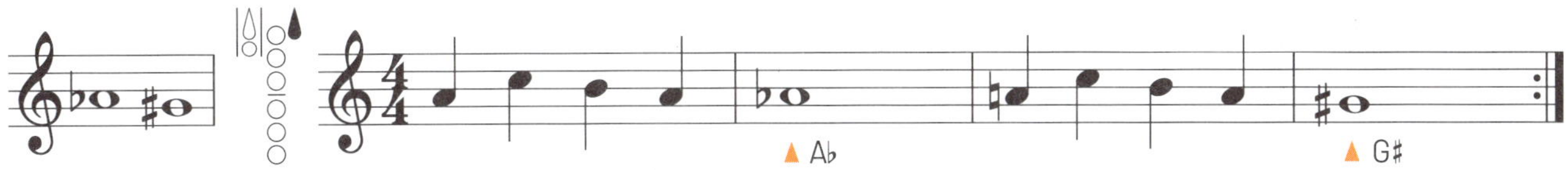


### 170. DARK SHADOWS

### 171. CLOSE ENCOUNTERS

*Enharmonic notes use the same fingering.*

**E♭/D♯**

### 172. MARCH SLAV

Peter Ilyich Tchaikovsky

### 173. NOTES IN DISGUISE

THEORY

## Chromatic Notes

**Chromatic notes** are altered with sharps, flats and natural signs which are not in the key signature. The smallest distance between two notes is a half-step, and a scale made up of consecutive half-steps is called a **chromatic scale**.

### 174. HALF-STEPPIN'

**F♯**

Alternate fingering

**HISTORY**

French composer **Camille Saint-Saëns** (1835–1921) wrote music for virtually every medium: operas, suites, symphonies and chamber works. The "Egyptian Dance" is one of the main themes from his famous opera *Samson et Delilah*. The opera was written in the same year that Thomas Edison invented the phonograph—1877.

### 175. EGYPTIAN DANCE *Watch for enharmonics.*

Camille Saint-Saëns

### 176. SILVER MOON BOAT

Chinese Folk Song

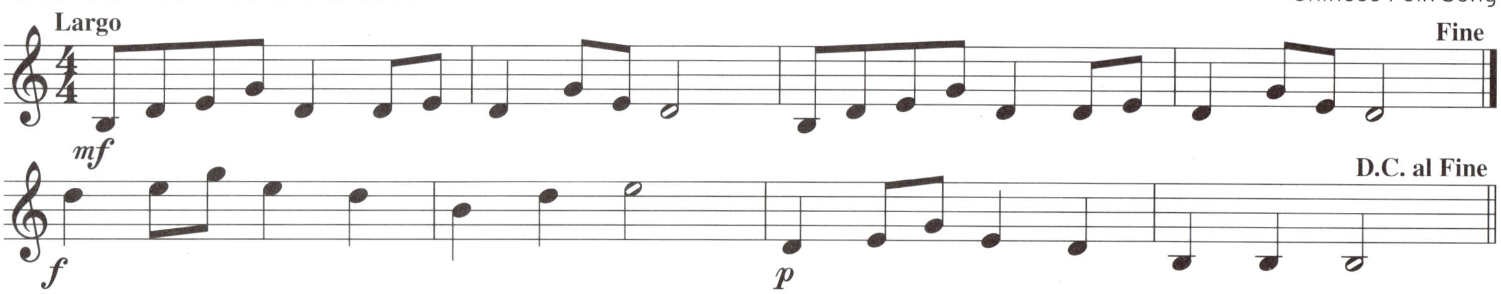


**HISTORY**

German composer **Ludwig van Beethoven** (1770–1827) is considered to be one of the world's greatest composers, despite becoming completely deaf in 1802. Although he could not hear his music the way we can, he could "hear" it in his mind. As a testament to his greatness, his *Symphony No. 9* (p. 13) was performed as the finale to the ceremony celebrating the reunification of Germany in 1990. This is the theme from his *Symphony No. 7*, second movement.

### 177. THEME FROM SYMPHONY NO. 7 – Duet

Ludwig van Beethoven

HISTORY

Russian composer **Peter Ilyich Tchaikovsky** (1840–1893) wrote six symphonies and hundreds of other works including *The Nutcracker* ballet. He was a master at writing brilliant settings of folk music, and his original melodies are among the most popular of all time. His *1812 Overture* and *Capriccio Italien* were both written in 1880, the year after Thomas Edison developed the practical electric light bulb.

## 178. CAPRICCIO ITALIEN *Always check the key signature.*

Peter Ilyich Tchaikovsky

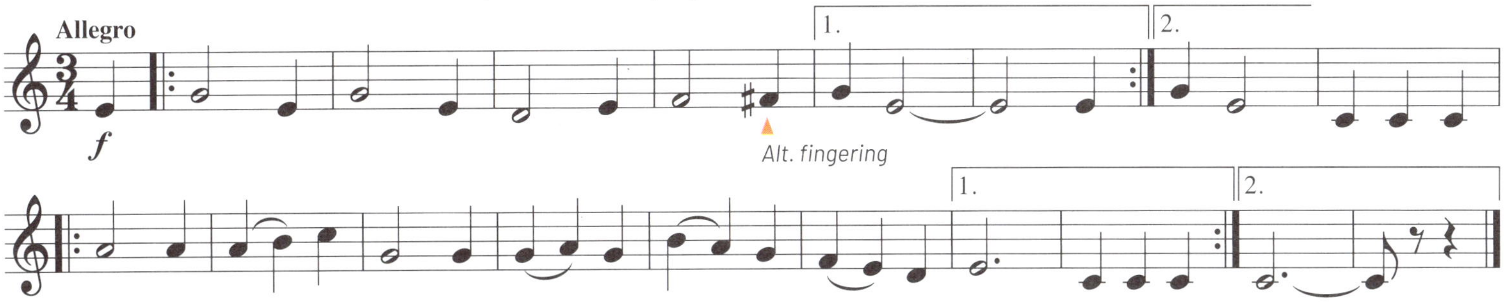


## 179. AMERICAN PATROL

F.W. Meacham

## 180. WAYFARING STRANGER

African-American Spiritual

## 181. ESSENTIAL ELEMENTS QUIZ – SCALE COUNTING CONQUEST

Additional bonus songs are available online. See the inside front cover for details.

# PERFORMANCE SPOTLIGHT

## 182. AMERICA THE BEAUTIFUL – Band Arrangement

Samuel A. Ward
Arr. by John Higgins

## 183. LA CUCARACHA – Band Arrangement

Latin American Folk Song
Arr. by John Higgins

# PERFORMANCE SPOTLIGHT

## 184. THEME FROM 1812 OVERTURE – Band Arrangement

Peter Ilyich Tchaikovsky
Arr. by John Higgins

# PERFORMANCE SPOTLIGHT

## Solo with Piano Accompaniment

Performing for an audience is an exciting part of being involved in music. This solo is based on *Serenade in G Major*, K. 525, also known as "Eine Kleine Nachtmusik" ("A Little Night Music"). **Wolfgang Amadeus Mozart** wrote this piece in 1787, the same year the American Constitution was signed into law. You and a piano accompanist can perform this for the band or at other school and community events.

### 185. EINE KLEINE NACHTMUSIK – Solo *(Concert B♭ version)*

Wolfgang Amadeus Mozart
Arr. by John Higgins

# DUETS

Here is an opportunity to get together with a friend and enjoy playing music. The other player does not have to play the same instrument as you. Try to exactly match each other's rhythm, pitch and tone quality. Eventually, it may begin to sound like the two parts are being played by one person! Later, try switching parts.

## 186. SWING LOW, SWEET CHARIOT – Duet

African-American Spiritual

## 187. LA BAMBA – Duet

Mexican Folk Song

# RUBANK® SCALE AND ARPEGGIO STUDIES

## CLARINET KEY OF C (CONCERT B♭)

**1.**

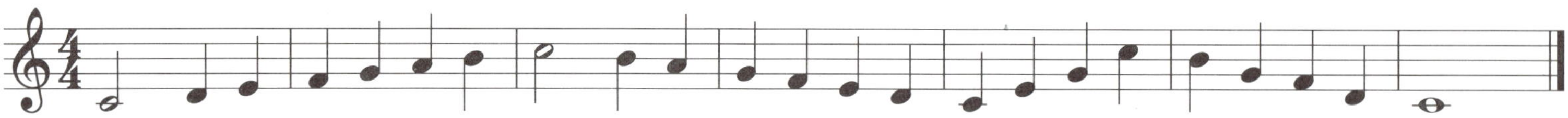

**2.**

**3.**

**4.**

## CLARINET KEY OF F (CONCERT E♭) *In this key signature, play all B♭'s.*

**1.**

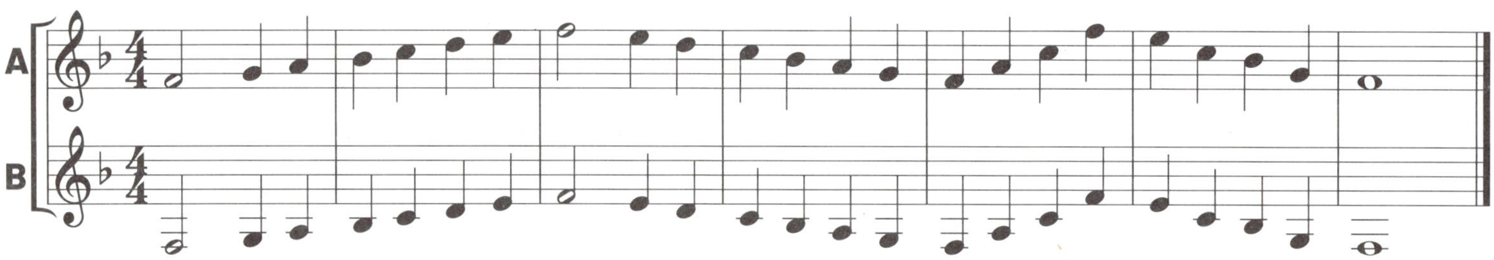


**2.**

**3.**

**4.**

# RUBANK® SCALE AND ARPEGGIO STUDIES

## CLARINET KEY OF G (CONCERT F) *In this key signature, play all F♯'s.*

**1.**

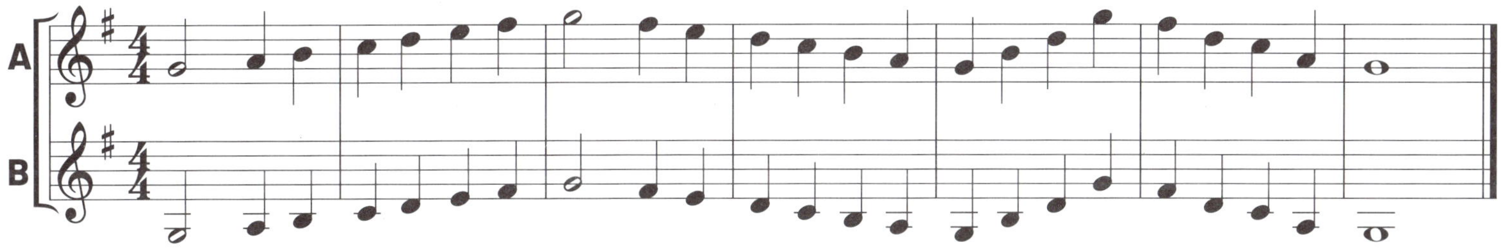

**2.**

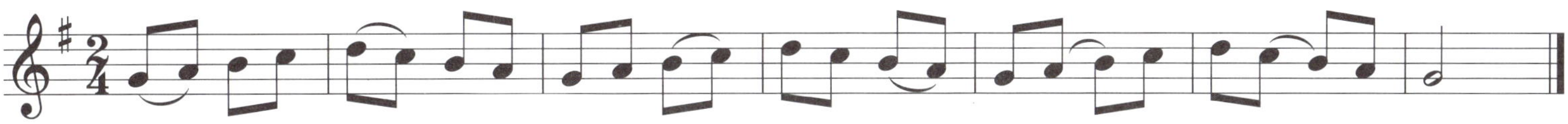

**3.**

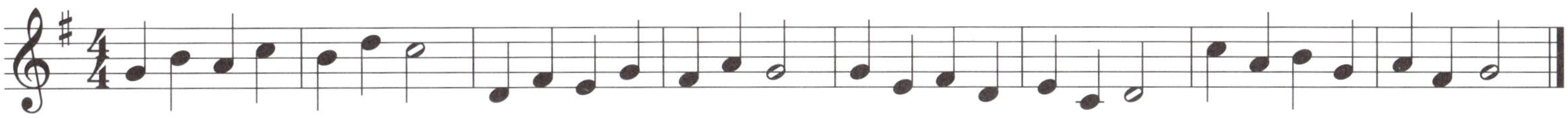

**4.**

## CLARINET KEY OF B♭ (CONCERT A♭) *In this key signature, play all B♭'s and E♭'s.*

**1.**

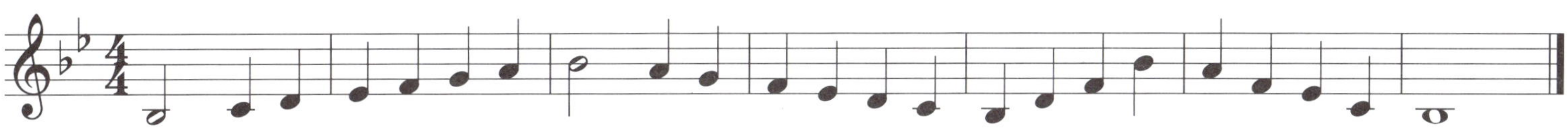

**2.**

**3.**

**4.**

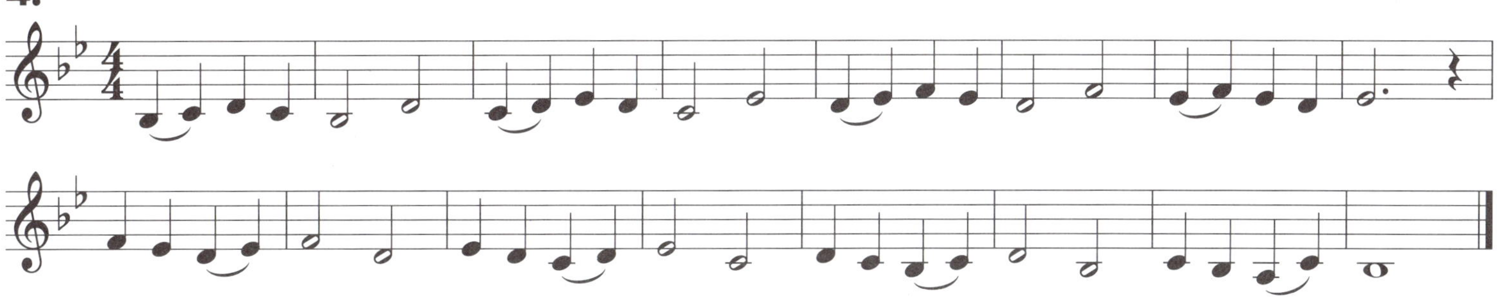

# RHYTHM STUDIES

# RHYTHM STUDIES

# CREATING MUSIC

THEORY

## Composition

**Composition** is the art of writing original music. A composer often begins by creating a melody made up of individual **phrases**, like short musical "sentences." Some melodies have phrases that seem to answer or respond to "question" phrases, as in Beethoven's *Ode To Joy*. Play this melody and listen to how phrases 2 and 4 give slightly different answers to the same question (phrases 1 and 3).

### 1. ODE TO JOY

Ludwig van Beethoven

### 2. Q. AND A.

*Write your own "answer" phrases in this melody.*

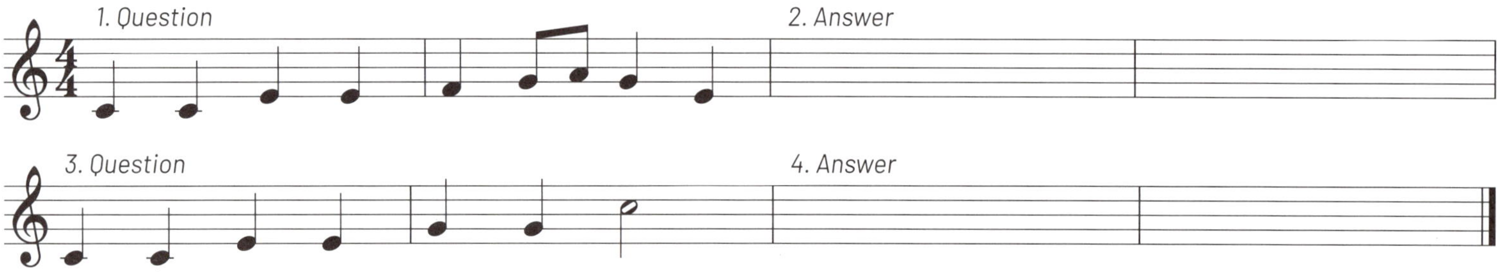


### 3. PHRASE BUILDERS

*Write 4 different phrases using the rhythms below each staff.*

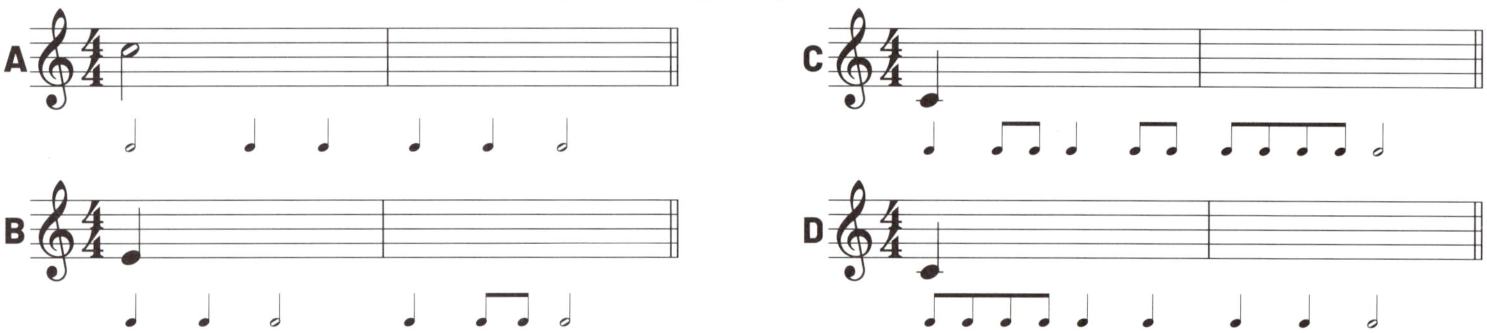


### 4. YOU NAME IT: ____________________

*Pick phrase A, B, C, or D from above, and write it as the "Question" for phrases 1 and 3 below. Then write 2 different "Answers" for phrases 2 and 4.*

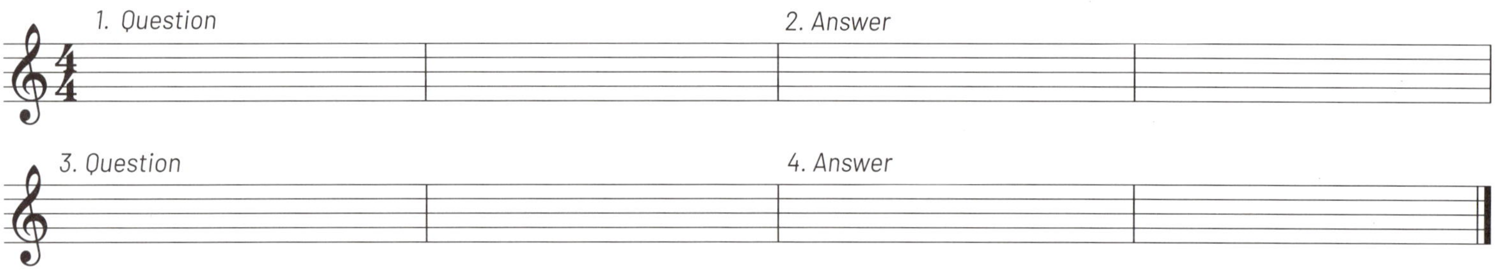


THEORY

## Improvisation

**Improvisation** is the art of freely creating your own melody *as you play*. Use these notes to play your own melody (Line A), to go with the accompaniment (Line B).

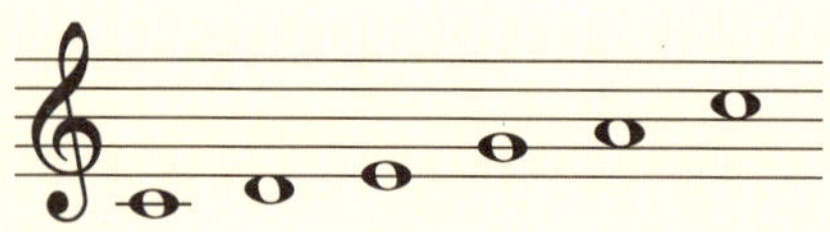

### 5. INSTANT MELODY

You can mark your progress through the book on this page.
Fill in the stars as instructed by your band director.

# ESSENTIAL ELEMENTS

## STAR ACHIEVER

NAME_______________________________

1. Page 2–3, The Basics
2. Page 5, EE Quiz, No. 13
3. Page 6, EE Quiz, No. 19
4. Page 7, EE Quiz, No. 26
5. Page 8, EE Quiz, No. 32
6. Page 10, EE Quiz, No. 45
7. Page 12–13, Performance Spotlight
8. Page 14, EE Quiz, No. 65
9. Page 15, Essential Creativity, No. 72
10. Page 17, EE Quiz, No. 84
11. Page 17, Essential Creativity, No. 85
12. Page 19, EE Quiz, No. 98
13. Page 20, Essential Creativity, No. 104
14. Page 21, No. 109
15. Page 22, EE Quiz, No. 117
16. Page 23, Performance Spotlight
17. Page 24, EE Quiz, No. 125
18. Page 26, Essential Creativity, No. 137
19. Page 28, No. 149
20. Page 28, EE Quiz, No. 151
21. Page 29, Performance Spotlight
22. Page 31, EE Quiz, No. 164
23. Page 32, EE Quiz, No. 168
24. Page 33, No. 174
25. Page 35, EE Quiz, No. 181
26. Page 36, Performance Spotlight
27. Page 37, Performance Spotlight
28. Page 38, Performance Spotlight

**MUSIC — AN ESSENTIAL ELEMENT OF LIFE**

# FINGERING CHART

**B♭ CLARINET**

## Instrument Care Reminders

Before putting your instrument back in its case after playing, do the following:

- Remove the reed, wipe off excess moisture and return it to the reed case.
- Remove the mouthpiece and wipe the inside with a clean cloth. Once a week, wash the mouthpiece with warm tap water. Dry thoroughly.
- Drop a weighted chamois or cotton swab into the bell and pull it out through the barrel.
- Carefully twist off the barrel and dry off any additional moisture. Place it in the case.
- Gently twist the upper and lower sections apart, with the bell still attached. Place the upper section in the case.
- Remove the bell and place the bell and lower section back into the case.
- As you put each piece back in the case, check to be sure they are dry.
- Your case is designed to hold only specific objects. If you try to force anything else into the case, it may damage your instrument.

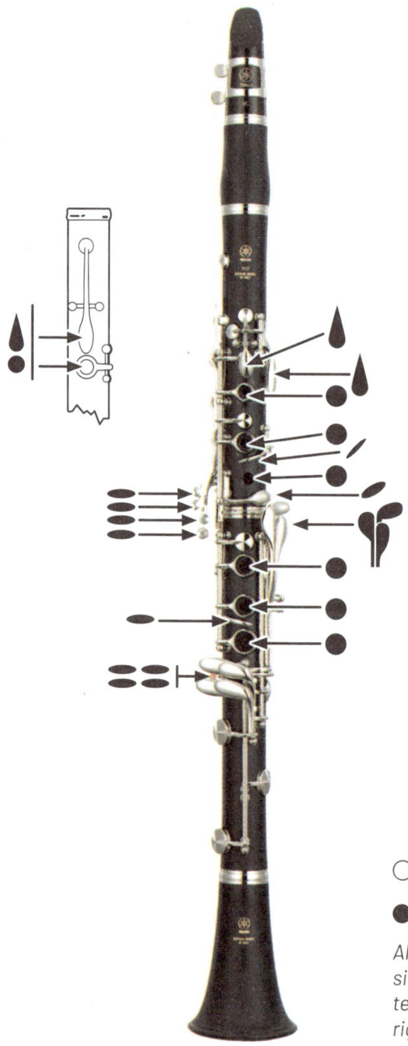

○ = Open

● = Pressed down

*Alternate fingerings are used in certain situations to allow for smoother technique. These are shown to the right of the more common fingerings.*

*Instruments and photos courtesy of Yamaha.*

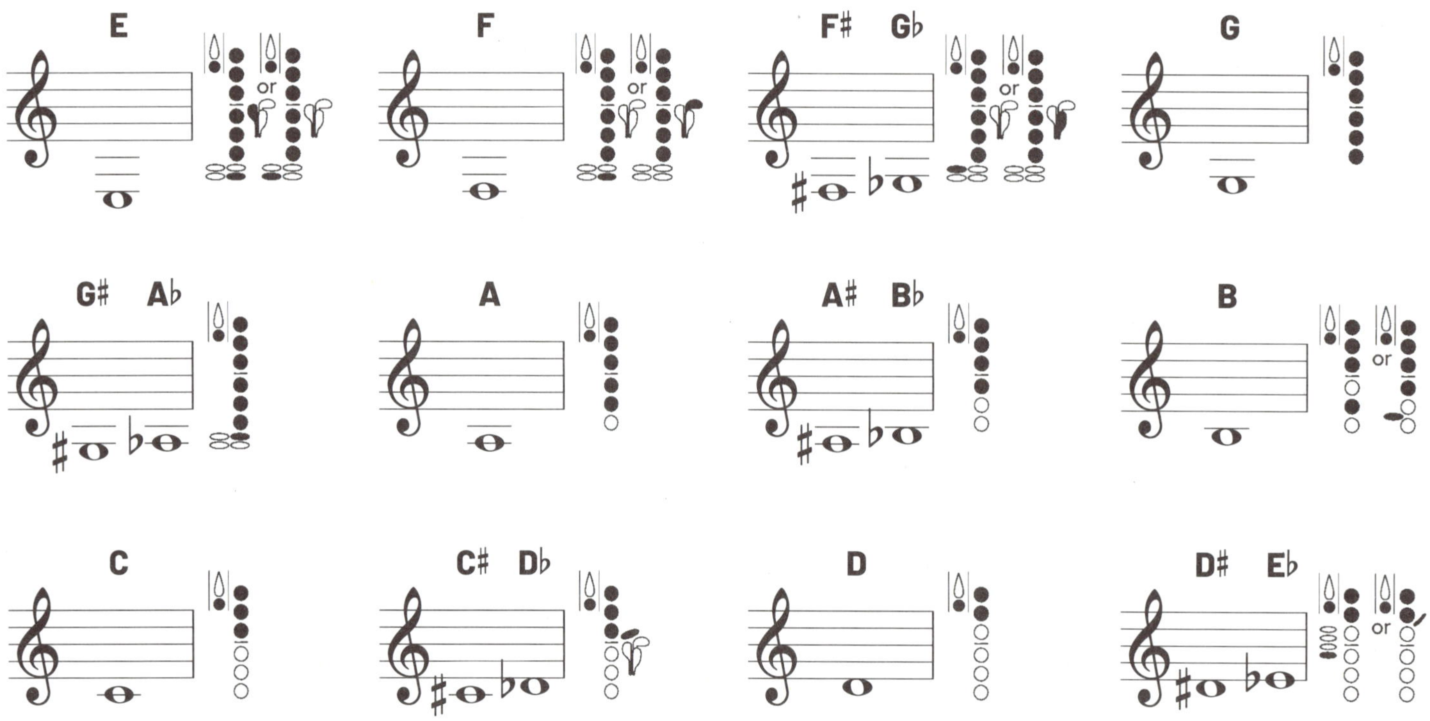

# FINGERING CHART

## B♭ CLARINET

# Reference Index

## Definitions (pg.)



## Composers



## World Music